Ethics for Accountants

Tutorial

Jo Osborne

Published by Osborne Books Limited
Tel 01905 748071
Email books@osbornebooks.co.uk
Website www.osbornebooks.co.uk

Design by Laura Ingham

Printed by CPI Group (UK) Limited, Croydon, CR0 4YY, on environmentally friendly, acid-free paper from managed forests.

British Library Cataloguing in Publication Data
A catalogue record for this book is available from the British Library

ISBN 978 1909173 835

Contents

Also available from Osborne Books...

Workbooks

Practice questions and assessments
with answers

Wise Guides

Handy pocket-sized study and revision guides

Student Zone

Login to access your free ebooks and
interactive revision crosswords

Download **Osborne Books App** free from the App Store or Google Play Store
to view your ebooks online or offline on your mobile or tablet.

www.osbornebooks.co.uk

Introduction

Qualifications covered

This book has been written specifically to cover the Unit 'Ethics for Accountants' which is mandatory for the following qualifications:

AAT Advanced Diploma in Accounting – Level 3

AAT Advanced Diploma in Accounting at SCQF – Level 6

The book contains a clear text with worked examples and case studies, chapter summaries and key terms to help with revision. Each chapter concludes with a wide range of activities, many in the style of AAT computer based assessments.

Osborne Study and Revision Materials

The materials featured on the previous page are tailored to the needs of students studying this unit and revising for the assessment. They include:

- **Workbooks:** paperback books with practice activities and exams
- **Wise Guides:** pocket-sized spiral bound revision cards
- **Student Zone:** access to Osborne Books online resources
- **Osborne Books App:** Osborne Books ebooks for mobiles and tablets

Visit www.osbornebooks.co.uk for details of study and revision resources and access to online material.

1 Principles of professional ethics

this chapter covers...

The aim of this chapter is to introduce you to the principles of professional ethics. We will look at what 'professional ethics' means and describe the fundamental ethical principles that members of the accounting profession should follow. These principles are followed in the 'Code of Professional Ethics' published by the AAT, which, like all professional accounting bodies' codes of ethics, is based on the IFAC ethical code.

Specific areas covered include:

- *the fundamental principles of professional ethics*

- *the people to whom these ethics apply*

- *the reasons why professional ethics are necessary*

- *the objectives of the accounting profession*

AN INTRODUCTION TO PROFESSIONAL ETHICS

what are ethics?

Firstly, a definition:

The professional ethics of an organisation are the moral principles or standards that govern the conduct of the members of that organisation.

You may have heard people refer to the fact that a person or an organisation has done something that is 'unethical', or that they themselves wouldn't do something because it was unethical. For example, you would consider it unethical for a doctor to give information to a newspaper about the treatment given to a celebrity patient without the patient's consent.

So why do we feel that this is unethical on the part of the doctor? In this case the doctor would have broken patient confidentiality – ie released information that is 'secret' and 'private' to that patient – and the doctor's actions would be considered unethical because of this.

Members of professional bodies are expected to maintain the standards of their organisation. As part of this they are expected to behave in a professional and ethical manner. Within the published rules and guidelines of most professional organisations there will be specific sections covering professional ethics. If you have online access, try doing a search on the phrase 'professional ethics for accountants' to appreciate how important the topic is.

professional ethics and the accounting profession

In the example above the doctor will be governed by the specific standards of the medical profession in the country in which he/she practises. However, as trainee accountants you are interested in the standards that affect you in your training and when you are qualified. As a professional body the AAT has published the **Code of Professional Ethics** which has been designed to help its members maintain the high standard of professionalism that is expected of them. Like all professional accounting bodies, the AAT Code is based on the International Ethics Standards Board for Accountants (IESBA)'s Code of Ethics. IESBA is the independent standard-setting board responsible for setting global ethical standards for accountants, and is part of the International Federation of Accountants (IFAC).

It is important to remember that compliance with the ethical code is a professional obligation rather than a legal obligation.

Decisions made by members of the accounting profession in their professional life can have real ethical implications. The Code is designed to help AAT members with these decisions. Specifically it states that it:

■ sets out the expected standard of professional behaviour

■ helps protect the public interest

■ helps to maintain the AAT's good reputation

In the same way members of other professional accounting bodies will be governed by their own ethical code.

Throughout this book we will examine in detail a number of possible areas where accountants are faced with ethical dilemmas and we will show how they should be dealt with ethically.

to whom does the AAT Code apply?

The AAT Code of Professional Ethics is an example of an accounting body's code of ethics. It applies to all fellow, full, affiliate and student members of the AAT. When applying for student membership the student signs a declaration agreeing to abide by the relevant regulations and policies of AAT. Therefore, as student members you are required to uphold the high professional standards of the accounting profession even before you have qualified and become a full member.

Some members of the accounting profession, when they become qualified, will decide to set themselves up in practice rather than continuing to be employed. Whilst the general ethical principles within the accountancy profession will be the same for members whether they are employed in business or in practice, there are a number of different legal and ethical issues that are specific to each group of members.

The AAT has recognised this and has separated the Code into three consecutive parts:

■ Part A applies to **all members**

■ Part B represents additional guidance which applies specifically to **members in practice** (ie one who works in an accounting practice that provides accounting and other services to clients)

■ Part C applies specifically to **members in business**

do you need to know the Code in detail?

You are not expected to have a detailed knowledge of the content of the AAT Code of Professional Ethics for your assessment. However, you are expected to have a clear understanding of professional ethics and be aware that the AAT Code and the ethical codes of other accounting bodies in the UK are based on the IESBA Code of Ethics.

OBJECTIVES OF THE ACCOUNTING PROFESSION

So far in this chapter we have identified that members of the accounting profession are expected to maintain professional standards with regard to professional ethics, and have described where guidance can be obtained. We will now move on to the objectives of the accounting profession (including the AAT).

The specific objectives of the accounting profession are shown in italics below. Each one is explained separately. There is no need for you to learn any of this wording. It is included here to give you some further information about why ethical behaviour is so important for accountants.

(i) *Mastering of particular skills and techniques acquired through learning and education and maintained through continuing professional development.*

As you will know from your studies, in order to become a member of any of the professional accountancy bodies, individuals must go through a demanding series of exams and assessments. This will normally involve a number of years of study linked to relevant training within the workplace, all of which is designed to ensure that the individual is fully trained to be a member of the accountancy profession and to take on the responsibilities of the role.

In addition to their training, qualified members of all the professional bodies are expected to keep their accounting knowledge up-to-date. One of the ways this is done is through **continuing professional development (CPD)**. As the name suggests, this involves accountants undertaking activities, such as attending seminars, to keep their knowledge and skills fully up-to-date so that they can carry out their jobs to the highest possible standards. We will look at CPD in more detail in Chapter 4.

An example where a member of the accounting profession requires some CPD follows.

example

the need for CPD

James Trebor is a professional accountant and has a successful practice preparing the financial statements of various local businesses. James completed his training in 2002 and although he is competent at what he does, he is not familiar with the new International Accounting Standards (IASs). In order to ensure that the accounts he prepares for his clients comply with the new standards, he has obtained copies of the IASs and has also arranged to go on an appropriate course run by his professional accounting body.

(ii) *Development of an ethical approach to work as well as to employers and clients. This is acquired by experience and professional supervision under training and is safeguarded by strict ethical and disciplinary codes.*

When training with a professional accountancy body, the most important thing is to pass your exams and assessments and to qualify. However, throughout your training you will also be learning from your supervisors and managers. Whilst this should obviously cover the processes and procedures involved in your job it will also teach you how to approach your work in a professional manner.

Managers who are qualified accountants should 'lead by example' and should ensure that all members of their staff work to the high standards expected of a professional accountant. As part of this they should be demonstrating strong ethical values and ensuring that they maintain the standards of the profession in their work and their dealings with clients.

For example, a manager who tells junior staff that 'it's okay to add a bit extra to their travel expenses claim because everyone does it' is clearly not acting in an ethical manner and is certainly not setting a good example for his or her staff.

(iii) *Acknowledgement of duties to society as a whole in addition to the employer or the client.*

It should be clear that professional accountants have specific duties in relation to their employers and, if they are in practice, in relation to their clients. In addition to this, the accountancy profession understand that they have a duty of care to the general public. Consequently, when they are carrying out their work they should always be aware of the wider picture and should consider the implications on society as a whole, as in the example which follows.

example

a duty to society

Whilst preparing the year-end accounts of Flexilock Plc, the accountant, John Bailey, has discovered that the company has been disposing of untreated chemical waste in a local river. John believes that this is illegal.

What should John do with the information that he has obtained?

John is in a difficult situation: he is employed by the company and does not want to risk his job. However, as a professional accountant he has a duty to society as a whole, who are likely to be harmed by the actions of the company. Initially John should raise his concerns with someone more senior in the company. If no action is taken John has an obligation to society and should report this information to the relevant authorities.

(iv)   An outlook which is essentially objective, obtained by being fair minded and free from conflicts of interest.

A person who is **objective** is someone who bases his/her opinions and decisions on real facts and is not influenced by personal beliefs or feelings. Accountants should always be objective. In addition, when they are faced with a conflict of interest, it is their duty not to let their own self-interest – or the interests of the firm that employs them – affect the professional decision that they make. The following example shows how a conflict of interest might arise.

example
a conflict of interest

Jill Saunders is in practice and has been the accountant for Stallone Ltd, a local firm of house builders, for a number of years. The company has two options for its next building project and the directors have asked Jill to draw up a business plan incorporating these options. The directors' preferred option involves purchasing a plot of land directly behind Jill's house and building 20 three and four bedroom houses. Currently Jill has unspoilt views from her house. There is clearly a conflict of interest here. Jill does not want the houses to be built behind her house and consequently can no longer be objective in these circumstances.

It is very important that Jill informs the directors of Stallone Ltd as soon as possible of this conflict of interest so that they are then able to make a decision as to whether they wish her to continue to prepare the business plan.

(v)   Rendering personal services to the highest standards of conduct and performance.

This objective can be looked at in two parts. Firstly, accountants must ensure that they carry out every piece of work to the best of their ability. They should allow sufficient time to complete the work, and should never 'cut corners' or compromise on the quality of the work performed. Secondly, accountants should ensure that they have the necessary skills to perform the work being undertaken. The following example shows how this objective may be compromised.

example
highest standards of conduct and performance compromised

Jasmine Chang was asked to prepare the accounts for Blue Truck Ltd. The Finance Director has asked that they be made available for the board meeting in two weeks time. Jasmine agreed to this timescale; however since then two junior members of her staff have been unwell and so have been unable to work. This has meant that Jasmine has had to prepare the accounts herself in addition to her own work.

Just before the board meeting the Finance Director noticed that the accounts appeared to contain a number of errors. He pointed this out to Jasmine who explained that she had been unable to check the detail in the accounts due to the pressures on her time. She knew that she should have spoken to the Finance Director as soon as she realised that the quality of her work might be affected by the shortage of time available to her to complete the assignment.

(vi) ***Achieving acceptance by the public that members provide accountancy services in accordance with these high standards and requirements.***

The accountancy profession is very focused on ensuring the highest standards from all its members. There is also the objective that accountants should be seen by members of the public to be working to achieve these high standards. In order for this to happen, the perception of the public must be that accountants are professional and trustworthy.

In recent years there have been a number of high profile cases where the standard of work that accountants have carried out has been called into question. The most famous of these is probably the collapse of the American energy company Enron. In 2002 the auditors of Enron, Arthur Andersen, were found guilty of obstruction of justice when there was evidence that they had shredded relevant documents immediately before the firm's collapse. Although this conviction was later overturned, the general public's perception of the accountancy profession was severely damaged by what they saw as highly unethical behaviour on the part of Arthur Andersen.

We can see that the accountancy profession, including the AAT, has set a number of demanding objectives for its members to commit to. In the next section we will describe how accountants can ensure that they achieve these objectives wherever possible.

FUNDAMENTAL PRINCIPLES

In order to achieve the objectives of the accountancy profession that have been explained above, a professional accountant is required to comply with a number of fundamental principles. Each of these is explained below, with practical examples. It is important to realise that many of the issues regarding professional ethics cannot be looked at on their own, but should be seen collectively. Where ethical issues arise, a number of the fundamental principles may be involved in any one particular case.

These fundamental principles can be remembered using the letters PPCIO, which also stands for 'Popular People Chat in Offices'. (See diagram at the top of the next page.)

integrity

Integrity is the quality of being honest and having strong moral principles that you refuse to compromise. An accountant should be straightforward and honest in all professional and business relationships and when carrying out professional work. Failing to act with integrity may mean that the accountant is directly or indirectly associated with misleading information. This could

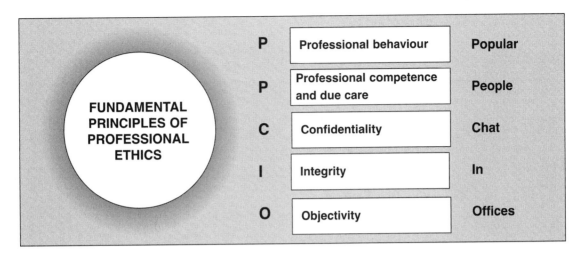

ultimately call into question his/her honesty and lead to users of the information such as clients, colleagues or even the general public no longer trusting the individual accountant or the accountancy profession as a whole.

There are also three key ethical values that contribute to the fundamental ethical principle of integrity: honesty, transparency and fairness. These are defined below.

- **honesty** – being truthful and trustworthy
- **transparency** – operating in a way that is easy for others to see what is being done or said
- **fairness** – acting reasonably and without bias

A professional accountant must ensure that he/she acts at all times with integrity, honesty, transparency and fairness whether he/she is dealing with clients, suppliers or colleagues.

The following situation is an example of where the integrity of an accountant might be tested.

example

a question of integrity

It is the end of the financial year and the Managing Director has told the Chief Accountant that he wants to maximise the profit for the year. He has asked the Chief Accountant not to set up an allowance for doubtful debts of £60,000 against an outstanding amount that the Chief Accountant knows is unlikely to ever be paid as the customer has recently gone into liquidation.

Clearly in this situation the accountant is faced with a difficult decision. He is employed by the company and consequently has a duty to the Managing Director. However, he knows that in order for the accounts to show the true position the debt should be provided against. In order to maintain his integrity in this situation the Chief Accountant should explain to the Managing Director that he is not prepared to ignore the doubtful debt and that in his opinion it should be provided for in the accounts.

objectivity

As a professional accountant the need to remain **objective** at all times is very important (see also page 7). This means that any decisions that are made should be based on real facts and should not be influenced by personal beliefs or feelings. The ethical code says that an accountant must not allow bias, conflict of interest or undue influence of others to override his/her professional or business judgement. Essentially, he/she must always act fairly and sensitively and without bias.

An example where the objectivity of an accountant could be affected is illustrated below.

example

a question of objectivity

Paula Gradwell is a Senior Accountant with a small local firm and is currently working on the year-end accounts of Bell & Sons. The owner, Alexander Bell, has asked Paula for her advice on whether the company should make a donation to the political party that he personally supports and how this will be treated in the financial statements. Paula has strong personal views against the party in question.

In this situation Paula must ensure that she remains objective when providing Alexander with advice. She must explain to him how any donation that Bell & Sons makes should be disclosed in the company's accounts. In this situation she must not let her personal opinions affect the advice that she gives.

professional competence and due care

The ethical code states that a member must act with '**professional competence and due care**' to maintain professional knowledge and skill at the level required to ensure that a client or employer receives competent professional service based on current developments in practice, legislation and techniques. A member shall act diligently and in accordance with applicable technical and professional standards when providing professional services.

If we first look at **Professional Competence**; professional accountants have a duty to keep themselves up-to-date with developments in the accounting profession, including relevant (international) accounting or auditing standards, and also regulatory and statutory requirements. The way in which they are expected to do this is by completing continuing professional development (CPD) on a regular basis, by reading current information on technical developments in the profession or attending relevant training courses.

The influence of international accounting standards is a specific example of the need for professional accountants to update their technical knowledge through training courses run by their own professional bodies.

Ideally, professional accountants should only take on new assignments for which they already have the necessary professional and technical skills. However, in certain circumstances, they may take on new work for which they will need some additional help or advice, as in the following example.

example

VAT expertise

One of your firm's clients has asked you to provide specific advice on the VAT implications of a new product imported from overseas. Although you have come across VAT as part of your accounting studies it is not something with which you feel particularly comfortable. So, what options are open to you in this situation?

1   You could decline the assignment on the basis that you are not suitably competent to carry out the work involved

2   You could employ someone with the appropriate skills to complete the work you cannot do, or subcontract the parts of the assignment you are unable to undertake

3   You could arrange appropriate training for yourself to enable you to carry out the VAT work that the client has requested

In each of the three options above, as a professional accountant you are ensuring that the work carried out is performed to the highest standards, either by someone else, or by you with additional training.

The second part of this principle is **Due Care.** This means that when carrying out an assignment an accountant must always take the appropriate amount of care (ie '**due care**') to ensure that the quality of the work performed meets the high standards expected of the accounting profession. Due care and diligence that are referred to in the ethical code mean acting in accordance with the requirements of the task: carefully, thoroughly and on a timely basis. Each assignment must be assessed individually in relation to its importance to the client and the time allowed for its completion. Whilst the work should be completed as quickly as is reasonably possible this should not compromise its quality.

Accountants must take particular care where clients are totally unfamiliar with anything to do with accounting or taxation. In such circumstances, accountants must be very careful to ensure that they carry out their work to the required standard. In addition to this they must also ensure that they explain fully to the client the results of the work that they have performed and the implications that this may have for the client.

For example, if two sole traders who do not seem to know much about accounting or taxation approach a professional accountant for financial advice as to whether they should go into partnership together, the accountant must ensure that he/she makes each of them fully aware of all the taxation and accounting implications involved.

confidentiality

The ethical codes states that members must comply with the principle of confidentiality

> '*to, in accordance with the law, respect the confidentiality of information acquired as a result of professional and business relationships and not disclose any such information to third parties without proper and specific authority unless there is a legal or professional right or duty to disclose. Confidential information acquired as a result of professional and business relationships shall not be used for the personal advantage of the member or third parties.*'

At the start of the chapter we introduced the example of a doctor who broke his patient's confidentiality by passing information to the press. All professions need to maintain confidentiality of client information. Accountants accumulate a large amount of information about their clients' affairs in the course of their work. Only in the most serious of circumstances, where there is a legal duty to disclose, would accountants be justified in revealing confidential information about their clients.

The example below raises the issue of **confidentiality**.

---

example

a question of confidentiality

You work for an accounting practice with a large number of clients in the local area. One Friday evening you have dinner with a good friend who explains that he has been offered a job with a local firm of publishers. He knows that they are one of your firm's clients and over dinner he asks you what their financial position is like and whether you feel that it would be a good move for him.

How should you deal with his questions?

In order to maintain the confidentiality of your client you should not disclose any information that is not already in the public domain. You should explain the need for confidentiality to your friend. You could suggest that he get the latest set of published accounts from Companies House which would give him an idea of the financial position of the company.

The subject of confidentiality and examples of situations when it can be broken are covered in detail in Chapter 5.

professional behaviour

The final fundamental principle is that of **professional behaviour**.

As we have seen earlier in this chapter the accountancy profession is respected for the high standards that it requires of its members. The ethical code states that accountants should '**adopt professional behaviour to**

comply with relevant laws and regulations and avoid any action that brings our profession into disrepute'. The whole of the ethical code sets out the required standards of behaviour that accountants should maintain and gives guidance on how to achieve them.

For example, a member of the AAT who sends offensive or inappropriate emails from their place of work would be considered unprofessional. In addition this could reflect very badly on the firm that he works for and also on the AAT.

A much more serious example of an accountant damaging the reputation of the accountancy profession would be if he or she gave professional advice to a client that the accountant knew failed to comply with relevant laws and regulations.

the importance of acting ethically

Whilst accountants have a professional duty to comply with the ethical code there are additional benefits of acting ethically.

- the code states that it helps protect the public interest; knowing that the accountant has a duty to act ethically will support the level of confidence that the public has in accountants
- an organisation that acts ethically will enhance its **probity** and reputation. Probity is the quality of having strong moral principles including honesty and decency
- an accountant that acts ethically will also enhance his/her professional reputation as potential clients and colleagues will have more confidence in an ethical accountant
- if an accountant acts ethically this will also help protect his/her legal liability

Chapter Summary

■ Members of all professional accounting bodies should maintain the standards of that organisation.

■ The professional ethics of an organisation are the moral principles or standards that govern the conduct of its members.

■ Accounting bodies base their code of ethics on the basic ethical code of the IESBA.

■ The accountancy profession (including the AAT) is committed to six objectives:

   – mastering skills and techniques through learning and training

   – developing an ethical approach to work and observing a code of ethics

   – acknowledging a duty to society as a whole

   – adopting an objective approach, free from conflicts of interest

   – providing accounting services to the highest standards

   – ensuring that the public knows that accountants provide services to these high standards

■ In order to achieve these objectives all accountants should observe the fundamental principles listed below.

The five fundamental ethical principles are:

   – integrity

   – objectivity

   – professional competence and due care

   – confidentiality

   – professional behaviour

Key Terms		
	professional ethics	the moral principles or standards that govern the conduct of the members of an organisation
	codes of professional ethics	documents issued by the accounting bodies providing guidance to full and student members regarding professional ethics
	integrity	accountants should be straightforward and honest in performing professional duties
	honesty	being truthful and trustworthy
	transparency	operating in a way that is easy for others to see what is being done or said
	fairness	acting reasonably and without bias
	continuing professional development	members of professional accounting bodies are expected to keep their technical knowledge up-to-date through relevant study, training and by attending courses
	objectivity	decisions should be made based on true facts and accountants must not let their own bias or prejudice, or pressure from others affect decisions that they make
	conflict of interest	these arise where the business or personal interests of an accountant may influence the accountant giving an objective opinion
	professional competence and due care	accountants have a duty to ensure that they have the necessary skills to carry out any work that is assigned to them and that they always take sufficient care to ensure that the quality of their work meets the high standards expected of them
	confidentiality	information obtained during the course of professional work should not be disclosed without proper and specific authority or unless there is a legal duty to do so
	professional behaviour	accountants should maintain the good reputation of the profession and should not do anything to discredit the profession
	probity	the quality of having strong moral principles of honesty and decency

Activities

1.1 Professional accounting bodies in the UK base their ethical codes on the Code of Ethics issued by which global body?

1.2 The AAT Code of Professional Ethics applies to which categories of member in the following list?

Tick any options that apply.

(a) Full AAT members	
(b) Student members of the AAT	
(c) AAT members who work in practice	
(d) AAT members who are employed in industry	

1.3 There are five fundamental principles of professional ethics with which professional accountants must comply.

State these **five** fundamental principles.

1.
2.
3.
4.
5.

1.4 The following statement is a definition of which fundamental ethical principle?

'Being honest and having strong moral principles that you refuse to compromise.'

1.5   The following statement is a definition of which fundamental ethical principle?

'Basing decisions on real facts rather than being influenced by personal beliefs or feelings.'

1.6   Complete the following statement:

'A professional accountant who complies with the law and does not bring the accounting profession

into disrepute is upholding the fundamental principle of [   ].'

2 Threats and safeguards to fundamental ethical principles

this chapter covers...

This chapter focuses on circumstances that create threats to the fundamental ethics principles of a professional accountant in practice and an accountant in business. It then details the safeguards that can be put in place to eliminate these threats or reduce them to an acceptable level. This chapter covers:

- *threats to the fundamental ethical principles of professional accountants in practice and in business, namely self-interest threats, self-review threats, familiarly threats, intimidation threats and advocacy threats*

- *safeguards against these threats for accountants in practice*

- *safeguards against these threats for an employed accountant in business*

- *safeguards created by the accounting profession, legislation and regulation*

THREATS TO FUNDAMENTAL ETHICAL PRINCIPLES

There will be circumstances in a professional accountant's working life, whether he/she works in practice or is employed in a business, where the accountant will face threats to the fundamental ethical principles. These threats will differ depending on the circumstances and whether the accountant works in practice or in business. However, the accountant must take a conceptual framework based approach to these threats and consider each individual circumstance when deciding how to deal with the threats he/she faces. In this chapter we will look at the types of threats faced by an accountant in practice and the safeguards that he/she can put in place to eliminate these threats, or reduce them to an acceptable level. We will then look at the threats faced by a professional accountant employed in business and the safeguards that can help to eliminate and reduce these threats.

THREATS TO THE FUNDAMENTAL ETHICAL PRINCIPLES FOR ACCOUNTANTS IN PRACTICE

A professional accountant who works in practice will face a number of potential threats to his/her fundamental ethical principles. These threats are summarised in the diagram below.

In the text that follows we will look at each of these types of threat in turn and identify situations where a professional accountant could be faced with a potential threat to his/her fundamental ethical principles.

potential threats to the fundamental ethical principles

'self-interest' threats

These may occur where a financial or other interest will inappropriately influence the accountant's judgement or behaviour.

'self-review' threats

These may occur when an accountant has to re-evaluate a judgement or data that he/she has previously made or produced.

'familiarity' threats

These may occur when, because of a close or personal relationship, an accountant becomes too sympathetic to the interests of others.

'intimidation' threats

These may occur when an accountant may be deterred from acting objectively because of real or perceived threats.

'advocacy' threats

These may occur when an accountant promotes a position or opinion (normally of a client) to the point that his/her objectivity may be compromised in the future.

self-interest threats

Where an accountant has a financial involvement with a client or in the affairs of a client, or in the operation of the business that employs him/her, this may threaten the objectivity of the accountant.

There are many examples of where the objectivity of a professional accountant may be threatened.

Set out below are several key areas where a financial involvement with a client or employer can arise. They are:

- direct or indirect financial interest in a client or employer
- loans to or from the client or any officer, director or principal shareholder of a client company or of an employer
- holding a financial interest in a joint venture with a client or employee(s) of a client
- when the receipt of fees from a client or group of connected clients represents a large proportion of the total gross fees of an accountant or the practice as a whole
- concern about losing a client
- potential employment with a client
- contingent fees relating to an assurance engagement
- discovering a significant error when reviewing previous work carried out by the accountant or a member of his/her staff

We will now explain these areas of financial involvement in more detail.

direct or indirect financial interest in a client or employer

If an accountant is a shareholder in a client company he/she would be considered to have a direct financial interest in that client. In this case the accountant's objectivity would be threatened as he/she would have a financial interest in the performance of the client business which could affect his/her judgement when preparing accounts or providing financial or tax advice. This self-interest threat would also extend to shares in a client held by a close relative of the accountant; for example, the accountant's husband or wife. The following example illustrates a situation of a self-interest threat resulting from a financial interest in a client.

example

shares in a client

Julie Parker is an accountant who works as a sole-trader and has a number of local firms as clients. Her husband Simon and his business partner are considering buying shares in a local business and have been considering investing in one of Julie's clients, Doors & Windows Ltd. Simon discusses this proposal with Julie over dinner one evening.

What points should Julie raise with Simon?

If Simon and his partner were to buy shares in Doors & Windows Ltd this would create a self-interest threat to Julie's objectivity. The financial success of the company would have a direct impact on the value of the shares that Simon and his partner held. This in turn would affect the financial position of Julie and her husband.

Julie should explain to Simon that this would be a threat to her objectivity. In this situation Julie and Simon have two choices: either Simon can go ahead with his partner and buy the shares, in which case Julie should resign as accountant for Doors & Windows Ltd. Alternatively, Simon should not go ahead with the planned purchase of shares in Doors & Windows Ltd.

loans to or from the client

If a client made a loan to an accountant who provided the client with accounting, taxation or other services, this could again affect the objectivity of the accountant. In this situation the client has financial influence over the accountant because of the money that is owed.

The example below illustrates a situation where this form of self-interest threat may arise.

example

loan from a client

Peter Moss is a professional accountant who runs a small but successful accounting practice. Peter is keen to expand the firm, and during an informal chat with one of his clients, he explains that he is considering moving to larger premises and employing more staff. He also explains that he will need to arrange a substantial loan with the bank to allow him to do this. A few days later the client telephones Peter and states that he would be willing to lend Peter the money to finance his proposed business expansion.

Should Peter accept the offer?

Peter should not accept the offer of a loan from his client. This would immediately create a self-interest threat to Peter's independence and so his objectivity through a financial involvement with the client. Peter should thank his client for the offer of the loan and politely say 'no, thanks'.

The only other solution would be for Peter to say to the client that he is no longer able to act as his accountant – but this is hardly realistic.

financial interest in a joint venture with the client

A self-interest threat would also arise for an accountant if he/she were to enter into a joint venture with a client or with an employee of the client. For reasons similar to those highlighted above, there would be a financial relationship between the client and the professional accountant which could compromise his/her independence. We return to the example of the accountant Peter Moss to show how this threat could occur in practice.

example

the threat of a joint venture

A few days after Peter declined the loan from the client explained in the example on the previous page, he receives a further telephone call from the same client. The client says that he has been thinking about what Peter has said and believes he has a solution where he could help Peter with his business expansion without providing him with a loan. His suggestion is that he and Peter's firm embark on a joint venture to purchase the premises. Peter's firm would continue to provide accounting services to existing and new clients. In return for his investment the client would expect a share of Peter's profits but would not be lending any money to Peter.

Should Peter now accept the offer given that the circumstances have changed?

Despite the changes in the nature of the offer, the client would still have a financial interest in Peter's firm and consequently there would be a self-interest threat to Peter's objectivity and so the offer should be politely refused. The only other solution, as before, is for Peter to resign as accountant for the client.

substantial fee income from a single client

If the fees that an accountant receives from an individual client represent a large percentage of the total gross fee income for the accountant (or his/her practice) this could again cause a self-interest threat to the accountant's objectivity. As the fee income from the client is so significant in relation to the accountant's total fee income this may well mean that the accountant cannot afford to lose the client which in turn could mean that the client has significant influence over the accountant.

example

the threat of substantial fee income

Sanjay Patel is a professional accountant who runs a successful practice providing accounting and taxation services to around 150 clients. His largest client, Emerson Ltd currently accounts for about 9% of his total fee income. Although Sanjay currently only provides accounting services to Emerson Ltd, the Managing Director of Emerson has asked whether he would like to take on the taxation work for the business. Sanjay estimates that the increased fees that this would generate would mean that Emerson Ltd would account for approximately 20% of his total fee income.

Should Sanjay agree to provide the additional taxation services to Emerson Ltd?

The total fee income from Emerson Ltd if Sanjay were to take on the taxation work would represent a substantial proportion of Sanjay's total fee income. This could represent a self-interest threat for Sanjay as he could become economically reliant on Emerson Ltd. Therefore in these circumstances, Sanjay should not accept the additional work that Emerson is offering him.

potential employment by a client

Inevitably when an accountant working in practice carries out an assignment for a client, the client will form an opinion of the ability of the accountant. In certain circumstances this may lead to the accountant being offered a job by the client. This could be as a financial accountant, a management accountant or in some other capacity. In this situation the potential employment of the accountant by the client could threaten his/her objectivity and professional behaviour when carrying out the assignment for the client. In order to protect his/her fundamental principles the accountant should immediately put safeguards in place. This could be by informing more senior members of staff on the assignment that a job offer has been or will soon be made or asking to be removed from the engagement team.

The following example illustrates the issue of a self-interest threat created by potential employment by a client.

example

the threat of potential employment

Zack is a professional accountant who currently works for a large accounting practice. He has been part of the team working on an assurance engagement for Pepperpot Ltd for the last three weeks. The Finance Director of Pepperpot Ltd has explained to Zack that they are currently looking for a senior accountant to work in his department and if Zack is interested the job is his. He also explains that the salary for the job is considerably more than Zack currently earns.

What should Zack do in this situation?

If Zack is not interested in the position he should politely decline the Finance Director's offer. However, if he is interested he must ensure that he puts safeguards in place to minimise the threat this might pose to his fundamental principles of objectivity and professional behaviour. He should explain the situation to his manager at the practice who should then decide whether to remove Zack from the engagement team or instead whether to fully review all of Zack's work. From a personal point of view Zack should also get a formal job offer from the Finance Director as soon as possible, ideally before he tells his manager!

contingent fees relating to an assurance client

A contingent fee means that the client will only have to pay the accountant if the work carried out results in an agreed outcome. When the work does not involve expressing an opinion, for example helping the client to prepare a bank loan application, it is acceptable for the fee paid to the accountant to be on a contingent basis, ie if the application is successful. However, if it is an assurance engagement a contingent fee could influence the accountant to give the appropriate opinion in order to secure his/her fee.

The following example shows how a contingent fee could result in a self-interest threat to a professional accountant's fundamental principles.

example

accepting a contingent fee

Sally, an accountant in practice, is discussing the fees that she will charge to one of her clients, Roger Porterich, for completing his profit calculation on which his tax return will be based. Roger suggests that he will pay Sally a higher fee provided the net profit figure is below £35,000. If the profit is over £35,000 she will receive a lower fee.

Should Sally accept the assignment on this contingent fee basis?

In this situation Sally is facing a self-interest threat to her objectivity as it is in her own financial interest to calculate a lower profit figure. In this situation Sally should explain this to Roger and ask that she be paid a set fee for carrying out the profit calculation regardless of the final value.

finding significant errors

On occasions an accountant working in practice will have to review or refer to work that has previously been performed by him/herself or by a member of his/her staff. If he/she finds a significant error in that work this could mean that he/she is faced with a difficult situation. Highlighting the error to the client could make the accountant or the member of staff appear incompetent. This could jeopardise the future relationship between the accountant and the client. This presents a self-interest threat to the accountant's objectivity and professional behaviour as the loss of the client would have a direct financial impact on the accountant's fee income. The alternative is not reporting the error to the client. This would threaten his/her fundamental principle of professional behaviour and also professional competence and due care.

Strong review procedures within the firm together with a leadership culture that stresses the importance of compliance with the fundamental principles will help to safeguard against this self-interest threat to the accountant's fundamental principles.

self-review threats

There is a threat to the fundamental principles of an accountant if a circumstance arises where he/she has to review his/her own work. This could be because the accountant used to work for the client and has now moved on to work for an accounting practice. Alternatively it could be because the accountant has moved from working for a practice into a role working for a client.

This type of threat to the independence of an accountant would also occur where the same situation applies to a close family member or colleague.

This self-review threat is illustrated in the following example.

example

a significant 'self-review' threat

Iris McDonald is a qualified accountant who worked for a number of years as Finance Manager for Catchett and Rank Ltd, a company that designs computer games.

After leaving the company Iris was employed as a senior manager by Michael Croft & Co, a local firm of accountants. A year after joining, Iris became a full partner in the firm.

Shortly after this she received a telephone call from a director of her previous employer, Catchett and Rank Ltd. He congratulated her on becoming a partner and explained that they were looking for some new tax advisors and thought that Michael Croft & Co might be a good choice.

Should Iris agree on behalf of Michael Croft & Co to accept the assignment?

Iris must use her professional judgement to decide whether it would be appropriate to accept the assignment. It would appear likely that in this circumstance she will have to review work that she has carried out and therefore there is a self-review threat. If it is possible for other members of staff at Michael Croft & Co to carry out the work so that Iris is not directly involved then it may be possible to reduce this self-review threat to an acceptable level. However, Iris must consider how the situation would appear to a reasonable and informed third party and whether he/she would consider her actions to be acceptable.

Other self-review threats to an accountant's fundamental principles:

- where an accountant discovers a significant error when reviewing work that he/she has previously carried out: he/she may decide not to highlight this error
- where an accountant is asked to report on the operation of financial systems after being involved in the design and implementation of these systems
- when an accountant performs a service for a client that directly affects the subject matter of the assurance engagement, for example when an accountant in practice prepares the depreciation calculation for a client and then is involved in the audit of the same client

If any of these self-review threats to an accountant's fundamental principles are present the accountant should identify appropriate safeguards to eliminate the threats or reduce them to an acceptable level. This could be by ensuring that his/her work is thoroughly reviewed by another accountant in the practice.

providing other services for clients

There may also be a threat to the fundamental ethical principles where professional accountants provide **consultancy services** to clients – eg management consultancy and tax advice – they must take care that they:

- make recommendations
- do **not** make management decisions
- do **not** take responsibility for management decisions

In this situation accountants should also avoid reporting on management decisions which they have recommended. Professional accountants should be independent advisors and not managers.

familiarity threat

Where a professional accountant has a close or personal relationship with the client or a key member of the client staff, this relationship may have a negative effect on the objectivity and the independence of the accountant. Because of this close or personal relationship an accountant may become too sympathetic to that person's interests.

The following example highlights a situation where such a relationship exists and the effect it could have on the independence of an accountant.

example

the threat of a family relationship

Liz Robinson is a professional accountant who owns and runs a small firm of accountants together with her business partner Tom Crusoe. She shares a house with her sister Jo who runs a successful training company. Up until now Jo has managed her own financial affairs, but her business is rapidly expanding and she can no longer manage the books herself. In addition, she has recently taken out a substantial business loan from her bank and, as part of the agreement, they have requested regular independently prepared financial statements.

Jo asks Liz if she will take on her business as a client. Should Liz accept this assignment?

There is a close family relationship between the two sisters which is made even closer by the fact that they share a house together. This close family relationship constitutes a familiarity threat to Liz's objectivity; consequently Liz should not agree to Jo's request and should instead recommend an alternative accountant to her sister.

In addition to the threat identified in the example above there are a number of other familiarity threats to an accountant's fundamental ethical principles. These include:

- where an accountant who was formerly partner of the accounting practice is now a director, officer or employee at the client in a position of significant influence over the subject of the assignment
- where an accountant is offered gifts or preferential treatment from a client unless the value of the gift is clearly insignificant; accepting gifts is covered in more detail in Chapter 3
- where there is a long association between a senior member of the assurance team and the client

In each of these circumstances the fact that there is a significant relationship between the accountant in practice and the client will pose a threat to his/her objectivity and potentially to his/her professional behaviour. Accepting a gift or preferential treatment from a client may influence the objectivity of the accountant, or equally important, it may appear to a person outside the accountant/client relationship that the accountant's objectivity is questionable.

As with all of the threats to an accountant's fundamental ethical principles the accountant must ensure that he/she puts sufficient safeguards in place to eliminate these threats or reduce them to an acceptable level.

intimidation threats

If an accountant takes on a client and a relationship develops in which the accountant is 'bullied' or put under pressure by the client – 'intimidated' in other words – then the objectivity of the accountant is under threat in a very real sense. As a result the accountant's reporting could be biased in favour of the client. In cases such as these, the accountant should be changed. If a larger firm is involved, a stronger personality could be brought into the accounting team to counter the client's threat to its fundamental principle.

Examples of intimidation threats include:

- the threat to dismiss by the client
- the threat by a client not to award a contract to the accountant
- the threat of litigation
- the pressure to reduce the quality of work in order to reduce fees
- the pressure to agree with the client's judgment because he/she has more experience of the matter in question

advocacy threats

Advocacy means that you are seen to support the client's point of view publicly – even in a court of law.

In the context of a threat to the fundamental ethical principles of an accountant in practice the advocacy threat is that the accountant could go beyond the **advisory** role that he/she should take for the client and **actively speak** on the client's behalf or in support of the client.

By promoting the client's position or opinion too strongly this may mean the accountant's objectivity in the future may be compromised.

The threat that this situation could pose is illustrated in the following example.

example

an advocacy threat to objectivity

Hugh Davies is a qualified accountant who provides a number of services to his clients, including accounting services, management consultancy and taxation advice. Over the past few months Hugh has been providing management consultancy services to Naturally Green, a company that sells organic and environmentally friendly products.

The directors of Naturally Green are in the process of updating their marketing brochures and have asked Hugh to provide a written statement, as management consultant, endorsing the product range that they sell.

Should Hugh agree to provide the requested endorsement?

If Hugh were to provide an endorsement of Naturally Green's products he would be going beyond his advisory role for the client and would be taking a strongly proactive stance on the client's behalf. This would have a seriously negative effect on Hugh's independence.

Consequently Hugh should refuse to provide the endorsement and should explain to the directors of Naturally Green the reasons for his refusal.

There are two more examples of circumstances that could create an advocacy threat to an accountant's fundamental principles. These are:

- promoting shares in a listed entity when the entity is an audit client
- acting as an advocate on behalf of an assurance client in litigation (legal cases) or disputes with another third party

An accountant must think very carefully before promoting a client or acting as the client's advocate. If there is any question in the accountant's mind as to whether his/her fundamental ethical principles are being threatened then he/she should decline to perform these roles for the client.

SAFEGUARDS AGAINST THREATS TO THE FUNDAMENTAL ETHICAL PRINCIPLES OF ACCOUNTANTS IN PRACTICE

How does an accountant in practice ensure that his/her fundamental principles and objectivity are maintained when accepting or continuing to work for a client? How does an accountant deal with threats to his/her fundamental ethical principles?

There are a number of possible safeguards and procedures that an accountant could put in place to help reduce the threats to his/her compliance with the fundamental ethical principles. These are in addition to any requirements provided for by law or by professional rules – for example the rules that govern the accountancy profession. A list of suggested safeguards is shown below. This list is not exhaustive, but it will help to summarise much of what has been explained in this chapter so far.

- a leadership culture in the accounting practice that stresses how important it is for staff to comply with the fundamental ethical principles

- a leadership culture in the practice that expects all members of staff working on assurance assignments to act in the public interest

- strong quality control procedures which are monitored for all engagements together with a member of senior management being given responsibility for overseeing the adequate functioning of this quality control system

- documented internal policies and procedures requiring compliance with the fundamental principles and a disciplinary mechanism to promote this compliance

- specific, documented policies for identifying threats to compliance with fundamental principles including evaluating the significance of these threats, and devising safeguards to eliminate these threats or reduce them to an acceptable level

- timely communication of a firm's policies and procedures, including any changes to them, to all partner and professional staff, and appropriate training and education on such policies and procedures

- documented independence policies for assurance engagements to ensure that the independence of members of staff is not threatened at any stage

- policies and procedures that will enable the identification of interests or relationships between members of staff and clients

- policies and procedures to monitor and, if necessary, manage the reliance on fees received from a single client

- using different partners on engagement teams with separate reporting lines to provide non-assurance services to an assurance client

- policies and procedures that prohibit individuals who are not members of an engagement team from inappropriately influencing the outcome of an engagement

- advising partners and professional staff of assurance clients that the practice and its members of staff must be independent from the client

- published policies and procedures to encourage and empower staff to communicate to senior levels within the firm any issue relating to compliance with fundamental principles that concern them

THREATS TO THE FUNDAMENTAL ETHICAL PRINCIPLES OF ACCOUNTANTS IN BUSINESS

Accountants in business will also be faced with threats to their fundamental ethical principles. As with accountants in practice these could be any of the following:

- self-interest threats
- self-review threats
- familiarity threats
- intimidation threats
- advocacy threats

We will now look at some examples of circumstances where these threats may occur.

self-interest threats

These threats may occur where financial interest on the part of the accountant may influence the judgement or behaviour of the accountant. Circumstances that could create self-interest threats for an accountant in business could be:

- an accountant having a financial interest in the business. For example an accountant may be entitled to compensation and/or incentives such as a bonus linked to his/her financial reporting and decision-making. As a consequence his/her objectivity may be threatened by this conflict of interest

- an accountant may have personal use of an asset of the business which is not part of his/her employment contract. This could create a self-interest threat to the objectivity of the accountant and also to his/her integrity and professional behaviour. For example, if an employed accountant was given use of his employer's corporate hospitality at an international cricket match and was able to take his whole family

- where there are concerns over the security of an accountant in business's employment which may threaten his objectivity

self-review threats

An accountant in business could face a self-review threat where he/she has been involved in preparing data that is then going to be used for making business decisions which the accountant is also involved in. For example an accountant may be asked to prepare the staff bonus calculations and then be involved in the decisions regarding who should receive these bonuses (this could also result in a self-interest threat if the accountant is eligible for a bonus).

familiarity threats

An accountant in business may face familiarly threats where he/she has a close personal relation which means the accountant becomes too sympathetic to the interests of that person or persons. There are several possible situations where a familiarity threat may arise:

■ where an employed accountant is preparing financial information for his/her employer which is the ultimate responsibility of an immediate or close family member this may pose a familiarity threat

■ where there has been a long association with a supplier or customer of the employer this could cause a familiarity threat

■ if an employed accountant is offered a gift or some other kind of preferential treatment by an employer, customer or supplier this could cause a familiarity threat to the accountant's fundamental principle as he/she may feel an obligation to conform to their wishes as a 'thank you for the gift'

intimidation threats

An employed accountant may feel intimidated and hence his/her fundamental ethics principles may be threatened in the following circumstances:

■ where there is a threat of dismissal to either the accountant in business or one of his/her close relations because the accountant will not conform to the wishes of his/her employer

■ where a dominant person in the employed accountant's business attempts to influence the decision making process by forcibly making his/her point

advocacy threat

As an employee of the organisation an accountant in business will be expecting to support the legitimate goals and objectives of the business. It would therefore, be part of the accountants job to promote the business provided, ensuring of course any statements that he/she made were not false or misleading. It is therefore unlikely that an employed professional accountant would be faced with an advocacy threat to his/her fundamental principles.

SAFEGUARDS AGAINST THREATS TO THE FUNDAMENTAL ETHICAL PRINCIPLES OF ACCOUNTANTS IN BUSINESS

In addition to the safeguards that are created by the accounting profession, legislation and regulation there are a number of safeguards that can be put in place in the work environment to reduce or eliminate the threats to the fundamental principles of a professional accountant in business. Examples of these safeguards are listed below.

- the employer's systems of corporate oversight or other oversight structures
- the employer's ethics and conduct programmes
- recruitment procedures that emphasise the importance of employing high calibre competent staff
- a system of strong internal controls
- appropriate disciplinary processes
- leadership within the business that stresses the importance of ethical behaviour and the expectation that employees will act in an ethical manner
- policies and procedures to implement and monitor the quality of training and clear training on these policies and procedures
- policies and procedures that encourage employees to communicate any ethical issues that concern them to senior management and also give them the power to do so without fear of retribution
- the opportunity to ask advice from another appropriate professional member of staff

SAFEGUARDS CREATED BY THE ACCOUNTING PROFESSION, LEGISLATION OR REGULATION

Previously we have said that in addition to the specific safeguards for accountants in practice and accountants in business there are safeguards created by the profession, legislation and regulations. These have been summarised again below.

- educational, training and experience requirements for entry into the accounting profession
- continuing professional development requirements
- corporate governance regulations
- professional accounting standards
- professional or regulatory monitoring and disciplinary procedures
- external review of the reports, returns, communications or information produced by a professional accountant by a legally empowered third party, for example an external auditor

In this chapter we have looked at possible threats to a professional accountant's fundamental ethical principles and safeguards that eliminate these threats or reduce them to an acceptable level. Where safeguards are put in place to reduce threats to an acceptable level then the decision to continue with the assignment must be documented. This documentation should include a description of the threats that have been identified and the safeguards that have been applied to eliminate or reduce them to an acceptable level.

But what if it is not possible to eliminate or reduce the threats to an acceptable level? If the accountant feels that even after the safeguards are put in place the threats are still clearly not insignificant then he/she must refuse to accept or continue working on the assurance engagement.

summary of the threats to fundamental principles

This chapter has looked at the threats to the fundamental principles that can face accountants in practice and also accountants in business. We have also identified the safeguards that can be put in place to eliminate these threats or reduce them to an acceptable level.

While all of the fundamental principles can be affected by any of the five types of threats, the table below summarises the particular threats of each fundamental principle. This table provides a handy revision summary for your synoptic assessment.

Threat / Principle	Self-interest threat	Familiarity threat	Intimidation threat	Self-review threat	Advocacy threat
Integrity	✔	✔			
Objectivity	✔	✔	✔	✔	✔
Professional behaviour	✔	✔		✔	
Professional competence and due care	✔	✔		✔	
Confidentiality	✔	✔	✔		

Chapter Summary

■ There are five main threats to the fundamental ethical principles of a professional accountant working in practice or in business which are:
  – self-interest threats
  – self-review threats
  – familiarity threats
  – intimidation threats
  – advocacy threats

■ There are a number of safeguards that accountants are able to put in place to eliminate these threats or reduce them to an acceptable level.

■ In addition to the safeguards that accountants can put in place to eliminate threats to their fundamental principles there are also safeguards created by the accounting profession, legislation or regulation.

■ Where safeguards will not reduce the threat to an acceptable level the accountant should refuse to accept or continue to work on the assignment.

self-interest threat to fundamental principles

the threat caused by a financial relationship between the accountant and a client or an employer

self-review threat to fundamental principles

the threat caused by an accountant having to review or evaluate a previous judgement that he/she has made

familiarity threat to fundamental principles

the threat caused by a close family relation or close friend of the accountant being a key member of the client staff or a supplier or customer of the accountant's employer

intimidation threat to fundamental principles

the real or perceived threat caused by a client exerting undue pressure on an accountant in practice or a dominant employer attempting to influence an accountant in business

advocacy threat to fundamental principles

the threat caused by an accountant going beyond an advisory role and publicly supporting the client in some way

Activities

2.1 Samantha is a professional accountant who works as a sole-practitioner. One of her larger clients, Red News has recently taken over one of its large rivals, Blue Media, which Red News intends to continue to operate as a separate entity. They have asked Samantha to take on Blue Media as a client. If she accepts this offer it will mean that the combined fee income from these two businesses will be 25% of her total fee income.

   (a) Explain which of Samantha's fundamental principles is most threatened by this situation and the type of threat that she is facing.

   (b) Should Samantha accept the additional work?

2.2 Complete the following statement by circling the appropriate word(s) for each option:

'When providing consultancy services to an existing client, professional accountants may face a **(self-interest/self-review/intimidation)** threat to their fundamental ethical principles. They must ensure that they **(do/do not)** make recommendations and **(do/do not)** make management decisions.

2.3 Hayley works for Trott & Cook. She has recently returned from a week's holiday to find a thank you card on her desk from one of her clients, Andrew. The card includes the following note together with a £150 gift voucher.

Hi Hayley,

Thank you for all your hard work on our financial statements this year. We are delighted that you decided not to raise the significant reduction in our allowance for doubtful debts with the management at Trott & Cook. This has meant that our profit figure for the year is in line with the forecast we gave our shareholders rather than much lower as it would have been without your help.

Please find enclosed a gift voucher as a small thank you.

Best wishes

Andrew

PS I would appreciate it if we could keep this arrangement between us as it may not look good for you if the partners at Trott & Cook found out about this.

(a)   If Hayley knowingly reduced the bad debt provision, explain which two of Hayley's fundamental ethical principles are most threatened by this situation.

(b)   What type of threat does Hayley face to her fundamental ethical principles?

(c)   If Hayley genuinely believed that the allowance for doubtful debts was correct are there any reasons that she cannot accept the gift voucher from Andrew?

2.4   Adrian has been employed by Tahil & Emerson, a medium sized accounting practice, since he started training as an accountant. He has now been qualified for four years. Each year since he joined the firm Adrian has been part of the team of accountants working on Tahil & Emerson's largest client, Headstyle Ltd, starting as a junior and currently working as the manager of the assignment. The Managing Director of Headstyle has asked Adrian if he would be interested in becoming the company's new Finance Director. He has asked that Adrian does not mention his offer until after the current year's assignment is complete.

(a)   State what types of threats Adrian is facing to his fundamental ethical principles.

(b)   Explain which two of Adrian's fundamental ethical principles are most threatened by this situation.

(c)   Explain what safeguards he can put in place to eliminate these threats or reduce them to an acceptable level.

2.5   Michael Austin works for Paragon Ltd, a company that manufactures industrial lighting. The managing director, Jules West, has recently leased a hospitality box at the local premiership rugby club for the whole season. Jules has said that Michael, a keen rugby supporter, can use the box for the cup final if he works late for the next week to ensure that the financial statements are completed on time.

(a)   Explain what type of threat Michael faces to his fundamental ethical principles.

(b)   Explain which two of Michael's fundamental principles are threatened in this situation.

(c)   What safeguards he can put in place to eliminate this threat or reduce it to an acceptable level.

2.6   Explain whether professional accountants in business or professional accountants who work in practice are more likely to face advocacy threats to their fundamental ethical principles.

3 Objectivity and the resolution of ethical conflict

this chapter covers...

This chapter explains the practical approach that a professional accountant takes to professional ethics and looks in more detail at objectivity and the need for an accountant to be independent. The chapter also deals with the way in which ethical problems can be resolved.

Specific areas covered include:

■ *the difference between a principles-based and a rule-based approach to professional ethics*

■ *acting ethically*

■ *the principles of objectivity including the acceptance of gifts or hospitality*

■ *the issues associated with inducements*

■ *the Bribery Act*

■ *the Fraud Act*

■ *ethical conflict including conflicts of interest and conflicts of loyalty*

■ *how to resolve ethical conflict*

A CONCEPTUAL FRAMEWORK APPROACH

what are the principles?

Chapter 1 of this book covered the fundamental principles of professional ethics. You may remember the mnemonic: **P**opular **P**eople **C**hat **I**n **O**ffices. This will remind you of the five fundamental principles of professional ethics:

- **P**rofessional Competence and Due Care
- **P**rofessional Behaviour
- **C**onfidentiality
- **I**ntegrity
- **O**bjectivity

The Code of Ethics sets out the fundamental ethical principles for members that provide a conceptual framework for dealing with ethical issues. In effect the ethical principles are the concepts that an accountant should adopt when dealing with an ethical issue.

The accounting profession believes that accountants should take a principles-based approach to professional ethics. This means that when faced with ethical decisions accountants should consider their decisions based on these fundamental principles rather than using a rigid system of rules and regulations.

We have seen that these principles are general in nature and so cannot be applied rigidly in specific situations to solve ethical problems that accountants come across in their working lives. When ethical dilemmas occur these principles should be considered together with the code of ethics. Accountants should use their professional judgement and consider the impact on their ability to act within the five fundamental ethical principles before any decision is reached on ethical matters.

principles-based approach

The code of ethics says that accountants should take a principles-based approach to ethics which requires an accountant to identify, evaluate and address threats to his/her compliance with the fundamental principles rather than applying a set of rules exactly as stated regardless of the circumstances (ie literally), which would be a rules-based approach. An example of a rules-based approach would be when you drive a car. You must follow the rules or you may cause an accident.

Put simply, this means that a professional accountant should evaluate anything that may prevent him/her following the fundamental ethical principles. If the principles are threatened then he/she should put safeguards in place to minimise the threat(s). We have already discussed these safeguards in Chapter 2.

The difference between a principle-based approach and a rule-based approach can be seen in the example that now follows.

example

principles-based approach v rule-based approach

Your firm of accountants has recently been taken on to provide professional accounting services for James Roberts, who is a self-employed painter and decorator. When preparing James's end of year accounts you realise that, early on in the year, the business's turnover has exceeded the annual limit for Valued Added Tax (VAT). This means that James should have registered for VAT and should from that point have been charging VAT on his services.

What should you do in this situation?

Taking a rule-based approach you would report James to HMRC for failing to register for VAT when his business had reached the VAT limit. This would arguably be a harsh course of action.

The preferred principles-based approach, on the other hand, would involve explaining to James that he must register for VAT immediately and should also make HM Revenue & Customs (HMRC) aware of the delay in registering that has occurred and the fact that he has not charged VAT on his services during the year as he should have done. Using this approach, you have identified the main issue – which is that James registers for VAT as soon as possible – and you have given James the necessary professional advice to allow him to do so.

acting ethically – not doing nothing

In the previous section we looked at how an accountant must take a principles-based approach to professional ethics. He/she must evaluate anything that may affect whether the fundamental ethical principles can be followed. However, they may be circumstances where it might be easier to simply ignore the problem or do nothing about it. But is this ethical behaviour by the accountant? The answer, is in most cases, it is not. If an accountant believes there is an ethical problem then he/she must take appropriate action in order to behave ethically.

The following example illustrates a situation where this might occur.

example

don't ignore the problem

Dustin is a management accountant who works in the accounts department of Vandex Ltd. Over lunch he is chatting with one of his colleagues, Lottie. Lottie explains that she has made an error on the firm's most recent VAT return that has resulted in Vandex Ltd underpaying HMRC by £2,000. She tells Dustin that 'no one seems to have noticed so she's not going do anything about it'. Dustin must now decide whether this situation is none of his business so he can ignore it or whether he should take some specific action.

In order to behave ethically Dustin cannot ignore what Lottie has said and do nothing about it, as this would be unethical. He must advise Lottie to report the issue to someone more senior in the accounts department and to correct the error on the next VAT return. If Lottie refuses to do this he should report it himself.

We will see later in the book in Chapter 6 that accountants are expected to take specific action to behave ethically when they encounter potential money laundering; another situation where the accountant cannot ignore the problem or do nothing about it.

acting ethically – complying with the regulations

We have established that it may not be acceptable for an accountant to ignore a problem or do nothing about it. In addition to this accountants cannot simply rely on complying with regulations as constituting ethical behaviour.

The example that follows shows how complying with regulations does not necessarily be behaving ethically

example

maternity pay

Marina plc has an employee grading system from 1-8 with 1 being the lowest paid workers and 8 being director level. The business's Maternity Policy states that eligible employees graded 1-4 who go on maternity leave will receive minimum Statutory Maternity Pay (SMP) as required by The Employee Rights Act 1996. However, the directors of the business have said that employees graded 5 and above will receive significantly better benefits and a large bonus when they return to work after their maternity leave has ended.

The fact that the directors of Marina plc are favouring the higher grade employees raises doubts about the ethical nature of the management and of its leadership culture. By simply complying with the SMP regulation they should not automatically be considered to be behaving ethically in relation to the business's employees.

A more ethical approach would be either to offer the minimum Statutory Maternity Benefit to all staff regardless of grade, or to offer improved benefits to all staff who go on maternity leave.

OBJECTIVITY

what is objectivity?

One of the fundamental principles covered in Chapter 1 is **objectivity,** which should be maintained at all times. A person who is objective has already been defined in Chapter 1 as someone who bases his/her opinions and decisions on real facts and is not influenced by personal beliefs or feelings or those of other people. The accountant must maintain a professional distance between his/her professional duties and personal life at all times. It is also important for an accountant to ensure that he/she collects all the information that is required before making any judgements.

If we now look at objectivity in more detail we can identify the key points that ensure that an accountant remains objective.

Firstly, in order to remain objective, an accountant should treat every situation equally and ensure that every point of view is given equal consideration (fair-minded). In addition to this the accountant should gather, analyse and present information accurately. To remain objective all accountants need to be free from conflicts of interest. This means that they must not allow their own self-interest or that of the organisation that they work for to influence any decision that they make.

independence

The principle of objectivity goes hand-in-hand with the need for independence. A definition of independence is **'freedom from control or influence of others'**. Often objectivity and independence are used interchangeably to mean the same thing.

An accountant must always carry out his/her work in an independent way and regardless of any external pressure. There may be people who try to put pressure on an accountant, or even make threats to try to ensure that the accountant's work is performed to best suit their needs. In order to act in a professional and ethical manner the accountant must not be influenced by this pressure and must remain independent, thereby protecting his/her fundamental principle of objectivity.

example

a question of independence

Amerdeep Johal works for a firm of accountants and is currently preparing the year-end accounts for ABP Supplies, a local company owned by two brothers Andrew and Brian Potter. Amerdeep has calculated a draft profit figure for the year of £56,000 compared with £127,000 in the previous year. During a meeting with the two brothers Andrew says that he is not happy with this profit figure as he has a meeting with the bank at the end of the week to discuss a loan and he knows they will be unhappy with such a large drop in profit. He asks Amerdeep if there is any way that he could 'improve' the profit figure.

Amerdeep explains that this would not be appropriate as the accounts would no longer give an accurate picture of the financial state of affairs of the business. Andrew replies that he will need to speak to the partner in the firm that Amerdeep works for who is a close friend of his and if this is not resolved he may consider changing the firm of accountants that ABP Supplies uses.

In this situation Amerdeep is being pressured by Andrew. Firstly, he will feel personal pressure as Andrew has threatened to speak to Amerdeep's boss. Secondly, he has threatened to take his business elsewhere which will have an impact on the firm that Amerdeep works for. In order to remain independent Amerdeep should not allow these pressures to influence him. He must stick to his principles and, provided his boss has the same ethical principles, Amerdeep should be confident that he will support him and will not expect Amerdeep to change his opinion.

Further emphasising the importance for professional accountants to remain independent, accountants must be both **independent of mind** and **independent in appearance**. We will now describe what is meant by these.

independence of mind

This means that when carrying out work and making decisions, a professional accountant should only take into account points and issues which are relevant to the job that he or she is doing. This is more or less the same as the principle of objectivity which we have discussed above. But in addition to being objective the accountant must be able to come to an opinion without his/her professional judgement being compromised.

In addition to this the accountant must ensure that he/she exercises a certain amount of **professional scepticism** when making a professional judgement. Professional scepticism is an attitude that includes the following:

- a questioning mind, ie not taking what is said at face value but instead asking questions until satisfied that the information is correct
- being alert to conditions which may indicate possible misstatement due to error or fraud, ie using professional experience and training to identify signs that a mistake has been made either as a result of a genuine error or due to deliberate fraud
- making critical assessment of evidence that is provided.

independence in appearance

In addition to maintaining objectivity and independence, an accountant must ensure that he/she is **seen to be** independent. This means that any reasonable person who comes into contact with the accountant must be confident that he/she always behaves independently and has avoided doing anything that may bring that independence into question.

The following example highlights a situation that may affect the **independence in appearance** of a professional accountant.

example

independence in appearance

Ashton and Groves is a small firm of accountants in Broom Town. One of the partners, Jemima Ashton, is married to Frank, who owns a local car dealership, Ashton Motors. For many years Ashton Motors have used Edwards & Co, another firm of accountants in the town, to prepare their year-end accounts. But Jim Edwards has just retired and Edwards & Co have ceased to operate.

Frank has suggested that the obvious solution would be for Ashton and Groves to take on the preparation of Ashton Motors accounts. But would this be appropriate?

The answer is no. Jemima, one of the Ashton & Groves partners, is clearly linked to the car dealership because she is married to Frank, its owner. Even if she had no involvement in the preparation of the accounts for Ashton Motors, her close personal relationship with Frank means that any outsider could quite justifiably question the independence and objectivity of Ashton and Groves.

safeguarding objectivity

There are a number of factors that will influence an accountant and safeguard his/her independence and objectivity.

- throughout their training professional accountants have been taught to act in a professional and ethical manner. They will be able to identify situations that could potentially affect their independence and they will be able to deal effectively with threats or pressures exerted on them

- an accountant should be aware of the possibility of legal action if he/she gives in to pressures that are exerted and allows his/her independence to be compromised

- members of any of the professional accounting bodies such as AAT, ICAEW, CIMA or ACCA, are aware of the possibility of professional disciplinary procedures against them from these bodies if they do not remain independent at all times

- finally, if an accountant is found to have compromised his/her objectivity and independence, this could potentially damage the accountant's reputation. The loss of professional reputation will often lead to the loss of clients and ultimately to loss of earnings

acceptance of gifts or hospitality

One possible threat to the objectivity of an accountant is the acceptance of gifts, services, favours or hospitality from a client. This is because there is a risk that these gifts could influence the work performed and decisions made by the accountant, effectively by bribing the accountant.

The problem here is whether all gifts or hospitality should be refused or whether it is acceptable to receive certain small gifts and favours. There is an argument that accepting a bottle of wine or some chocolates from a client at Christmas will not influence an accountant's work or opinions. However, would this still be the case if the gift was a case of wine? At what point would it no longer be appropriate to accept such gifts?

The following example illustrates this issue.

example

Merry Christmas!

Simon Fuller works for Adams & Co, a firm of accountants in Bridgetown. During the week before Christmas, Sara, one of the owners of Peroni, a local restaurant which is one of the firm's clients, turns up at the office with a crate of champagne. Sara hands it to Simon together with a Christmas card and wishes him a Happy Christmas. She suggests that he gives a bottle to each member of staff. Sara says 'tell Roger Adams that I've arranged the table for your firm's Christmas party on Friday and not to worry about the bill as it's on Peroni!'

What are the ethical implications of this situation? Should Simon Fuller accept the champagne and should Adams & Co accept the offer of a free Christmas meal from Peroni?

With regard to the champagne it is unlikely that if each member of staff accepts a bottle of champagne this will influence their objectivity when working on the accounts of Peroni. The acceptance of a free Christmas meal, however, is another matter. This is likely to mean a substantial cost saving for Adams & Co. If a third party was aware of this they may consider that Adams & Co could be influenced by the financial benefit that they are getting by not paying for the meal. Even if the owners of Peroni say that they do not expect anything in return, Adams & Co should decline the offer, enjoy the meal and ensure that they pay for it in full.

From this example it can be seen that there are no rules regarding what is and what is not acceptable. A professional accountant must use professional judgement and experience to decide whether he or she is allowed to accept gifts from a client. In most cases, however, if there is any question in the accountant's mind he or she should politely refuse a gift from a client.

INDUCEMENTS

Having looked at the ethical issues for an accountant in practice surrounding accepting gifts and hospitality from a client, there is a similar issue for employed professional accountants. An **inducement** is something that is offered to encourage or motivate a person to do something. Inducements may take various forms, including, gifts, hospitality, preferential treatment or even friendship!

Such inducements offered to an accountant could create a threat to his/her compliance with the fundamental ethical principles. The objectivity or confidentiality of an accountant can be threatened when an inducement is made in an attempt to:

- influence actions or decisions
- encourage the accountant to act dishonestly or illegally
- obtain confidential information

If an accountant is concerned that inducements could threaten his/her adherence to the fundamental principles he/she should assess the risks and decide what action should be taken. Options are:

- immediately inform higher management
- inform a third party of the offer, for example, a professional body such as the AAT (the accountant should also consider taking legal advice before doing this)

- tell a close friend, colleague or relation if they are likely to benefit from the inducement and

- inform higher management in the organisation for which the person works

The following example illustrates the issues associated with inducements.

example

an issue of inducement

Uma is an accountant who works as a management accountant for Pentagon Ltd. It is just before the company's accounting year-end on 31st March. Her manager, Simeon, calls her into his office and explains that the company's results are not as good as he had hoped. As his bonus is based on achieving a certain level of profit he is quite concerned. He asks Uma to raise a number of fictitious invoices dated immediately before the year-end to boost the sales and the profit figures for the year. He will then authorise credit notes to be raised against these invoices in the new financial year. In return for doing this Simeon says he will give Uma £1,000.

What should Uma do in this situation?

Simeon has offered Uma a financial inducement to do something dishonest. Uma has two options:

1   Uma could go to the Finance Director and tell him what Simeon has said, although there is a possibility that he may actually have asked Simeon to make the offer to her.

2   Uma could inform her professional accounting body of the offer that Simeon has made. However, as this is a serious step to take, she may want to take legal advice before doing so.

compromised objectivity

In this chapter we have looked in more detail at the fundamental ethical principle of objectivity. But what happens if an accountant's objectivity is compromised by a gift or an inducement? The risk for the accountant is that he/she could be accused of **fraud** or of **bribery**. We will now look at each of these possible accusations.

fraud

Fraud can be defined as 'wrongful or criminal deception intended to result in financial or personal gain.' An accountant who accepts a gift or an inducement will gain from it financially and/or personally. If this is seen by a third party to affect the objectivity of the accountant it could result in the accountant being accused of fraud.

The **Fraud Act 2006** defines three classes of fraud:

- fraud by false representation – where a person makes any representation which they know to be misleading

- fraud by failing to disclose information – where a person fails to disclose any information to a third party which he/she has a legal duty to disclose

- fraud by abuse of position – where a person occupies a position where they are expected to safeguard the financial interest of another person, and abuses that position

bribery

The **Bribery Act 2010** covers the criminal law relating to bribery. A definition of bribery is:

> *'Giving or receiving something of value with the intention of influencing the recipient to do something favourable to the giver of the bribe.'*

A person that offers an inducement to another person for the improper performance of a function or activity is guilty of the offence of bribery. Equally a person who is willing to accept that inducement can also be prosecuted under the Bribery Act. The four key Bribery Act offences are:

- bribing another

- receiving a bribe

- bribing a foreign official

- failing to prevent bribery

The maximum penalty if a person is found guilty of the offence of bribery is 10 years imprisonment and/or an unlimited fine. There is also the potential for property to be confiscated.

ETHICAL CONFLICT

ethical conflict between interests of different clients

In Chapter 1 we discussed the issue of **conflict of interest** in relation to the objectivity of an accountant, explaining that accountants should not allow business or personal interests to prevent them from remaining objective and independent. The interests here are clearly those of the **accountant**.

Another situation where a conflict of interest can occur relates instead to the interests of the accountant's **clients**. Accountants who work in public practice normally have a significant number of different clients. Consequently there is a strong chance that at some point there may be a conflict of interest between two or more, of these clients. For example the accountant may have a number of clients which work in the same market sector, all competing for the same customers so the success of one client in increasing sales may well have a negative effect on another client in the same sector.

The issues for an accountant who is working for clients where a potential conflict of interest exists are predominantly those of objectivity and confidentiality.

There are two potential problems which the accountant may face:

■ the accountant may provide services and give professional advice to one client where he/she knows that this will have an adverse affect on another of his/her clients (objectivity)

■ information gained about one client could potentially be beneficial to another and vice versa (confidentiality)

In many cases, the risk associated with these issues can be reduced to an acceptable level by compartmentalising the responsibilities and knowledge about each of the clients by using different members of staff to work on the client assignments. However, if this safeguard does not reduce the threat to the fundamental principles to an acceptable level then the accountant should not accept or continue one or more of the appointments.

When an accountant is considering taking on a new client or where there are any changes in the circumstances of existing clients the accountant should take all reasonable steps to find out whether a conflict of interests exists or could arise.

If a significant conflict of interest is identified between clients, the accountant should ensure that the clients involved are fully informed of the circumstances. This will then allow each of them to make an informed decision about whether to use the accountant's services.

The issue of conflict between the interests of different clients is illustrated in the example that follows.

example

a conflict of interest

Jim Kirk is an accountant who runs Kirk & Co. a successful firm of accountants in Pineridge. Jim has recently been approached by Robert Redpool, one of the partners in Blackwell & Redpool, a local firm of builders asking if Kirk & Co. would be interested in carrying out some accounting work for them relating to the potential purchase of a development site in Pineridge. One of Jim's existing clients, Bluebell & Whitelake is also a building firm located in Pineridge.

What points should Jim consider when deciding whether to accept the assignment for Blackwell & Redpool?

First, Jim must investigate whether there could be a conflict of interest between the potential client and his existing client, Bluebell & Whitelake. If he believes that there is, or could be, a conflict of interest between the two clients, Jim must then decide whether Kirk and Co. have sufficient staff to use separate staff on each of the clients. This would reduce the risk that the interests of either client could be adversely affected if Kirk & Co. took on the new work.

If Jim believes that he can adequately safeguard the interests of both clients he should then contact Blackwell & Redpool and Bluebell & Whitelake and fully explain the situation, including the staffing measures Kirk & Co. intends to put in place. This will then allow the existing client and the potential client to decide for themselves whether they are happy to enter into, or continue in, a relationship with Kirk & Co.

If Jim decided that he could not sufficiently reduce the risks associated with the conflict of interest between the two builders, then he must either decline the appointment with Blackwell & Redpool (the more likely option) or end Kirk & Co.'s relationship with Bluebell & Whitelake.

In this circumstance he must ensure he fully documents the process he goes through.

conflict of loyalties for an accountant

a definition of loyalty

One definition of loyalty is:

> *'being firm and not changing in your support for a person or an organisation, or in your belief in your principles.'*

Society generally views loyalty as a good thing whether it is to friends, family or to employers. Employers are keen for their employees to be loyal to the organisation that they work for as this encourages stability within the workforce and a good team spirit, which in turn contributes to the success of the organisation. It also means that employees will be supportive of decisions taken by the organisation that they work for and will carry out the tasks that are expected of them.

One of the factors that will help to maintain an employee's loyalty to the organisation that he/she works for is a culture that encourages strong ethical values. We have seen in previous chapters just how important the accounting profession considers ethics to be for its members. But this need for strong ethical values is not limited to the accountancy profession. Every employee, regardless of their seniority in an organisation, should maintain an ethical approach to their work.

conflict of loyalties

Employed accountants are expected to be loyal to their employer; but, as professional accountants, they also owe a duty of loyalty to the accounting profession. There is potential for conflict here. As an employee it would seem logical that the employed accountant's first priority should be to support his or her organisation's objectives and the rules and procedures drawn up in support of them, provided that the organisation is acting in a legal and ethical way. However, there may be times when something that the employer expects the professional accountant to do conflicts with his/her professional and ethical values.

Because of the responsibility to his/her employer, an accountant may be put under pressure not to comply with the fundamental ethical principles. He or she may face pressure to:

- break the law

- breach the rules and standards of their profession

- be part of a plan for unethical or illegal earnings

- lie or mislead (including by keeping silent) auditors or regulators, or

- put their name to or otherwise be associated with a statement which materially misrepresents the facts

We can see that all of the above are very serious situations. Each one clearly conflicts with the ethical standards expected of a professional accountant.

Breaking the law is obviously not something anyone, never mind a professional accountant, should do. The rules and standards of the accounting professional are clearly there for a purpose and should not be broken by members of the profession. Note that breaching ethical standards includes not only active deception, but also an accountant misleading auditors by just keeping quiet when he/she knows the auditors have got something wrong.

So what happens if an employed accountant is put in a position where the employer puts pressure on him/her to do one (or more) of the above? Possible action that the accountant could take can be summarised as follows:

- if the employer has broken the law, the accountant should try hard to persuade the employer not to continue with the unlawful activity and to rectify the situation as soon as possible

- if there is a difference of opinion between the accountant and the employer regarding an accounting or ethical matter, wherever possible this should be resolved with the involvement of more senior staff within the organisation. If necessary, the issue should be dealt with using the employer's formal dispute resolution process

- where the issue between the employer and the accountant cannot be resolved and the accountant considers that he/she has exhausted all other possible alternatives then he/she may have no option but to offer to resign. In this case the employed accountant should explain to the employer the reasons for his/her resignation, and should at the same time maintain the duty of confidentiality to the employer

It is worth noting here that the accounting profession and the code of ethics strongly recommends that the employed accountant should obtain advice from his/her professional body or legal advice before taking the step of offering to resign. One important reason for this is that the law now protects an employee from dismissal for 'whistleblowing', ie breaking confidentiality. In other words, the employee should not have to be put in the position of having to lose his/her job when the matter is serious enough to be made public. Only the employed accountant's professional body or a lawyer (or both) can advise in this situation.

The process of dealing with conflicts of loyalty is summarised in the diagram below.

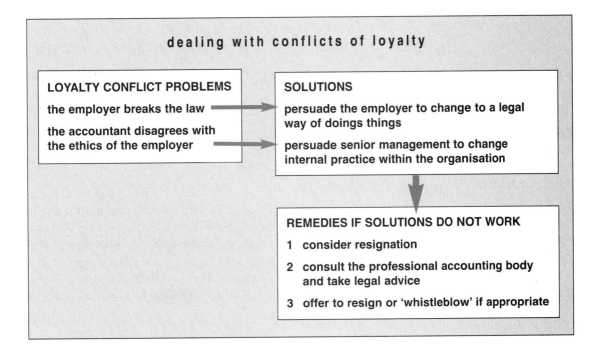

dealing with conflicts of loyalty

LOYALTY CONFLICT PROBLEMS

the employer breaks the law

the accountant disagrees with the ethics of the employer

SOLUTIONS

persuade the employer to change to a legal way of doings things

persuade senior management to change internal practice within the organisation

REMEDIES IF SOLUTIONS DO NOT WORK

1 consider resignation

2 consult the professional accounting body and take legal advice

3 offer to resign or 'whistleblow' if appropriate

The area of conflict of loyalties and the ethical issues that it raises is illustrated in the example that follows.

example

a conflict of loyalties

Rona Hughes works as an Accounts Assistant in the accounts department of Peters & Son where one of her responsibilities is to prepare the quarterly VAT Return for the company. It is now the end of the financial year and the Financial Controller has asked Rona to manipulate the figures to be included on the VAT Return so that the company's year-end VAT liability is reduced.

This is clearly wrong and Rona should take no part in the Financial Controller's request to falsify the data that is to be included in the VAT Return. But what should she do in these circumstances to resolve the problem?

As an employee of Peters & Son, Rona has a duty of loyalty to the company and to the Financial Controller as her line manager, but she also has a duty to follow the rules and regulations of the accountancy profession and adhere to the fundamental principles of professional behaviour, professional competence and due care and integrity.

In this case there is a conflict of loyalty between the two. In the first instance, Rona should explain to the Financial Controller that she has serious concerns about doing what he has asked and cannot be involved in such activities. If, at this point, the Financial Controller agrees with Rona that she is right, then no further action needs to be taken. However if, despite raising her concerns with him, there is still a disagreement, Rona would have to raise the issue with a higher level of management.

Finally, if Rona has no success when she raises the matter with the senior management of Peters & Son and the Financial Controller continues to falsify the VAT records, Rona will be faced with no alternative but to consider resigning. Before doing so she should take relevant legal advice.

If, after taking legal advice, she decides that resigning is the only course of action available to her, Rona should explain her reasons for resigning to the management at Peters & Son. She will still be bound by her duty of confidentiality to her employer and so should not tell anyone else these reasons at this stage.

the problems raised by conflict of loyalties

You will see that a number of issues are raised by the example of Rona Hughes above. Firstly, she has been put in a very difficult position as a result of the request made by the Financial Controller. He is more senior than she is and so has the authority to put pressure on her to comply with what he has asked her to do. Raising the issue with more senior management in the organisation is likely to cause a significant amount of tension between the Financial Controller and Rona, which could ultimately make her position within Peters & Son very difficult.

Resigning from the company would also be a huge step for Rona to take. The consequences of this could be that she may not receive a reference from Peters & Son, or may find it difficult to find another job.

With all these issues to contend with it is easy to see why some employees choose to remain silent about malpractices that occur within their organisation. They choose instead, to 'keep their heads down' and ignore the ethical issues that this raises.

ETHICAL CONFLICT RESOLUTION

There will be occasions in an accountant's working life when he/she may be faced with an ethical conflict in the application of the fundamental principles. In these circumstances the accountant will need to find a method for resolving this conflict. If the organisation that the accountant works for has a formal conflict resolution process (as many large professional accounting firms do) the best approach may be to use this conflict resolution process. Alternatively the accountant may initially try to resolve the conflict informally.

In either case when attempting to resolve the conflict the accountant should consider each of the following points:

- the relevant facts relating to the conflict

- assess all the ethical issues involved

- the fundamental principles that are involved by the ethical conflict to the matter in question

- whether there are established internal procedures to deal with the conflict and if so how they can be applied to the situation

- what alternative courses of action are available to the accountant

- seek advice from others

Having considered these factors, the accountant will need to decide the best course of action that is consistent with the fundamental principles identified. He/she will also need to consider the consequences of each possible course of action. If the ethical conflict remains unresolved, the accountant may decide to consult with other appropriate colleagues for help finding a resolution. Where an issue is raised with a line manager the accountant must ensure that this is done discretely and confidentially.

If, after consulting with a colleague, the accountant is still unable to resolve an ethical dilemma or ethical conflict the accountant may decide that he/she needs to seek further advice. If the organisation that the accountant works for is large enough this may initially be from the employer's ethics helpline. However, for accountants employed in smaller organisations they may need to contact the helpline of their professional accounting body. The AAT has a confidential Ethics helpline that is available to give advice to its members.

If the ethical conflict is between the accountant and another member of staff or the organisation that he/she works for the accountant may need to report this to the persons charged with governance (management) of the business for resolution. This may be the Board of Directors or the Audit Committee.

The accountant must remember that it is always important to document the details of the ethical issue involved together with details of any discussions held or decisions taken, concerning this issue.

The following example illustrates how an ethical issue could be resolved using this approach.

resolving an ethical conflict

a taxing question

Ben works as a manager for Parkinson & Norton, a large accounting practice. One of the partners, Michael Norton, has asked him to personally carry out some taxation work for a client, Ricard Dupre. During the work on Ricard's tax return Ben realises that Ricard is currently setting up a new business venture with another of Ben's clients, Jon Darmery. There are some issues in Ricard's tax affairs that indicate to Ben that Jon may not be fully aware of Ricard's true financial position.

Ben is now faced with an ethical dilemma. Should he break confidentiality rules and tell Jon what he has found out about Ricard or risk compromising his professional competence and due care?

Although Ben may be tempted to go straight to Michael Norton, he should do the following:

- gather all the facts relating to the situation
- assess the ethical principles involved, in this case professional competence and due care and confidentiality
- decide what procedures (formal or informal) are available within Parkinson & Norton for the resolution of ethical conflicts. This could be reporting the issue to a senior member of staff or, if there are legal issues involved it may require external advice
- decide what alternative courses of action are available and the consequences of each one. This could involve explaining to Ricard that Parkinson & Norton has an issue as they already act for Jon Darmery and matters arising from their review of Ricard's affairs mean their professional competence has been compromised. It could also be to advise Ricard to fully disclose his financial affairs to Jon or to give Parkinson & Norton authority to disclose the information
- he should then discuss the issue with Michael Norton and document the results of the discussion and the course of action that has been decided upon, He must be sure that whatever decision is finally made it does not compromise his fundamental ethical principles and those of Parkinson & Norton

The above example identifies an ethical dilemma for an accountant in practice who is dealing with a client. However, there may be occasions when an accountant is faced with an ethical dilemma when dealing with a supplier. For example, if a supplier offers to carry out work for the business on a cash basis so that the business avoids paying VAT and the manager of the business accepts the offer. This would create an ethical issue for the accountant. In this case he/she would have to take the same approach detailed on the previous page to resolve the ethical conflict.

failure to resolve an issue

If an ethical conflict cannot be resolved, a professional accountant may consider obtaining professional advice from his/her professional accounting body or taking legal advice. This would have to be done on a confidential basis and to ensure that there was no breach of confidentiality.

An example of where this confidentiality issue might arise would be if the accountant suspects that a fraud may have been committed by a colleague, employer or client. In this case he/she may need to discuss confidential information with advisors from his/her professional accounting body or a lawyer to confirm whether his/her suspicions are justified. It should be noted that in this example of suspected fraud the accountant may then have to consider having to submit a report to NCA or to his/her employer's Money Laundering Reporting Officer (MLRO).

Ultimately if the accountant is still unable to resolve the ethical conflict, he/she may have to dissociate him/herself from the issue. This could be by withdrawing from the engagement team working on client assignment or actually resigning altogether from the engagement, the firm that he/she works for or the employer.

Chapter Summary

- When ethical decisions need to be taken, the conceptual framework means that a principles-based approach should be adopted, based on the objective to be achieved rather than applying the rules exactly as stated.

- Accountants must follow the principle of objectivity which is key to professional accountants remaining independent.

- When making decisions, an accountant must ensure that he/she remains independent of mind and only take into account issues and points that are relevant to the issues that they are addressing.

- In addition to independence of mind, the accountant must demonstrate independence in appearance. This means that they should avoid situations that could make a third party question the accountant's objectivity.

- Accountants must ensure that they put safeguards in place to protect their objectivity.

- A professional accountant must use his or her professional judgement to decide whether to accept gifts from a client.

- If an accountant is offered an inducement to influence his/her behaviour this may threaten the objectivity or confidentiality, or both, of the accountant.

- If an accountant is concerned about being offered an inducement he/she should inform the appropriate person.

- Where ethical conflicts arise, accountants should take all necessary steps to resolve these, and if necessary should seek advice from a solicitor or from their professional accounting body's advice line.

- The Fraud Act 2006 defines three types of fraud: fraud by false representation, fraud by failing to disclose information and fraud by abuse of position.

- The Bribery Act 2010 is the UK legislation covering the criminal offence of bribery.

- Where conflict of interest exists between two or more clients, an accountant should take all possible steps to minimise the risks that could arise.

- Employed accountants have a duty of loyalty to the organisation that employs them and also to the accounting profession. On occasion these different loyalties may conflict.

Key Terms		
	conceptual framework	a set of principles to help accountants to act ethically
	principles-based approach	this means to use the conceptual framework to identify and evaluate threats to the fundamental ethical principles and put in place safeguards to minimise or eliminate these threats
	rule-based approach	the approach to professional ethics that means that you apply any rules exactly as stated regardless of the circumstances
	objectivity	not allowing personal beliefs or feelings or pressure from others to affect decisions that are made
	independence of mind	only taking into account points that are relevant to decisions to be made or work that is being undertaken – this is very similar to objectivity
	independence in appearance	ensuring that to a third party the actions taken by the accountant appear to be objective and free from the influence of others
	professional scepticism	an attitude that includes a questioning mind, being alert to conditions which may indicate possible misstatement due to error or fraud, and a critical assessment of evidence
	inducement	something offered to encourage or motivate a person to do something
	bribery	giving or receiving something of value with the intention of influencing the recipient to do something favourable to the giver of the bribe
	fraud	an intentional deception made for professional gain or to damage another individual
	loyalty	being firm and not changing in support for a person or an organisation
	conflict of loyalties	this arises where an employee's loyalty to his/her employer clashes with his/her loyalty to the accounting profession
	ethical conflict	this occurs where there is a fundamental disagreement between what has been requested of the accountant and what his/her ethical principles indicate that he/she should do

Activities

3.1 'Taking an approach that identifies, evaluates and addresses threats to compliance with the fundamental ethical principles.'

To which of the following does this approach to professional ethics relate?

Tick **one** option.

(a) A rules-based approach	
(b) A principles-based approach	

3.2 Babridge Limited employs a number of staff in its warehouse. These warehouse workers have recently been required to do a significant amount of overtime to fulfil an urgent overseas order. Overtime worked is paid to all staff in the business at their standard hourly rate. The Managing Director has decided to give the sales team that secured the order a large bonus in addition to their overtime but does not plan to give bonuses to the warehouse staff.

Decide whether each of the following statements is true or false.

	True	False
(a) Because staff are paid for the overtime that they work Babridge Limited is automatically considered to be behaving ethically towards its staff		
(b) The Managing Director's decision regarding staff bonuses raises concerns about the ethical nature of the management and leadership of Babridge ltd.		

3.3   Wanda is a professional accountant who works for Ashby & co, a medium sized firm of accountants. She has recently finished assignments for two clients, Arthur Price, who owns a chain of exclusive cake shops in the north of England and Jayne Meeson, who is the owner of a local car dealership.

The following two matters have arisen this week.

A hamper filled with cakes, biscuits and other luxury food has arrived at the offices with a note from Arthur Price. The note says:

> Hi Wanda,
>
> Thanks for all your hard work on my accounts this year, you and your team were a pleasure to have at our office. Please feel free to share these goodies amongst your staff.
>
> Best wishes,
>
> Arthur

An email from Jayne Meeson has arrived in Rhona's inbox. The email says:

> Hi Wanda,
>
> Thanks for all your hard work on our accounts and tax affairs this year; we really enjoyed having you and your team here during your visit.
>
> I know you are keen to buy a new car soon so I would like to offer you a 50% discount on any quality used car we have in stock. Please let me know when you will be in to look around!
>
> I look forward to hearing from you soon.
>
> Kind regards
>
> Jayne

(a)   Explain which of Wanda's fundamental ethical principles may be threatened by these matters.

(b)   In each of these situations what is the best course of action for Wanda?

3.4 If a professional accountant in business is offered something beneficial to him/her to encourage the accountant to do something this is known as what?

3.5 Saul works for Geronimo Ltd, a technology company in Bandridge. His girlfriend, Emma, is an accountant who for works for Lone Ranger, a company that makes computer games. The Managing Director of Lone Ranger has recently announced that he wishes to retire and is looking for a buyer for the company.

The Managing Director at Geronimo has asked Saul to find out from Emma what sort of price she thinks her Managing Director will accept for the business. He adds that Saul and Emma will be most welcome to use his holiday cottage in Devon if his bid for Lone Ranger is successful.

(a) Identify which of Saul and Emma's fundamental ethical principles are threatened by this situation.

(b) What action could Saul take in these circumstances?

3.6 What is the maximum penalty if a person is found guilty of the criminal offence of bribery?

3.7 Terry is a qualified professional accountant who has worked for Parks & Co for a number of years. Over the last three years Terry has been involved on the assignments for two large local building firms, Pentagon Homes and Vale Housing. A large building plot that has space for 100 houses has recently come up for sale and both Pentagon Homes and Vale Housing are putting in a bid for the land. They have each asked Terry to act for them in relation to the bid. Both building firms have now realised that the other is likely to be interested in the land. Pentagon has offered Terry an additional fee of £5,000 to act for Pentagon Homes only, meanwhile Vale Housing has offered £6,000 if Terry will act exclusively for them. Neither of the companies is happy for Terry to act for both building firms in relation to the bid.

(a) Which two of Terry's fundamental principles are threatened by the fact that both Pentagon Homes and Vale Housing are both bidding for the same piece of land.

(b) What process can Terry go through to resolve the ethical conflict he has in deciding how to deal with this situation?

(c) If Terry decides to act for one of the clients explain two issues that he must consider when carrying out the assignment.

3.8   Esther is a professional accountant who works for Goodrich Ltd. The Accounts Department are currently preparing the year-end financial statements and part of Esther's responsibilities is to prepare the inventory valuation. Esther attended the year-end inventory count and identified £60,000 of inventory that is not in saleable condition and will need to be scrapped. She has highlighted this to her manager, Sam, and suggested that £40,000 should be written off the inventory value.

Sam told Esther that he does not want her to write off the damaged inventory and they will deal with it after the year-end. The total value of the inventory before this £40,000 proposed reduction for damaged stock is £347,000.

(a)   Explain the conflict of loyalties that Esther faces in this situation.

(b)   What options does Esther have to deal with this conflict of loyalties?

Professional and technical competence

this chapter covers...

This chapter explains the need for a professional accountant to adhere to the fundamental principle of professional and technical competence. It details the ways in which an accountant can attain professional competence and how to maintain it. It also looks at the critical areas where an accountant needs to have up-to-date technical knowledge.

The next section of the chapter deals with the need for professional accountants to work within their capabilities and what to do if they are asked to carry out work beyond their competence. Finally it looks at professional liability, disclaimers of liability and indemnity insurance.

PROFESSIONAL COMPETENCE

Before taking on a new client or embarking on a new piece of work, an accountant must make sure that he/she has the ability to carry out the work involved and the necessary technical and professional competence to complete the job.

There are two separate issues which relate to an accountant's competence. First of all, the accountant must gain (attain) professional competence. Secondly, the accountant must ensure that he/she maintains professional competence. We will now explain each of these in turn.

attaining professional competence

Most people who are reading this book will be studying to become a member of the AAT and will probably be working in an accounting related job. By the time all the training, assessment and examinations have been successfully completed to allow a person to become a member of the accounting profession this should mean that they have gained the necessary professional competence.

maintaining professional competence

This is not, however, the end of the training for a professional accountant. Regardless of the professional body which has awarded the qualification, there is a requirement to maintain a level of professional competence. Accountants must keep **up-to-date** with all new developments in the accounting profession: as you know from your studies in other units accounting standards are constantly changing both nationally and internationally. Accountants are required to keep up-to-date with all these changes, together with any other relevant amendments to auditing standards or other legislation such as changes in taxation laws.

up-to-date technical knowledge

It has already been mentioned that professional accountants must ensure that they have up-to-date technical knowledge to ensure that they can act with technical and professional competence when providing services to clients and carrying out duties for their employer. We will now look at the areas in which it is important for an accountant to maintain up-to-date technical knowledge. We will then look at the ways in which the accountant can keep up-to-date.

critical areas

Accountants must ensure that they maintain their professional competence in all areas of accounting and finance that they work. There are some particular areas in which this up-to-date technical knowledge is critical. We will now look briefly at each of these.

■ **changes in financial reporting and auditing standards**. International Financial Reporting Standards (IFRSs) are issued by the International Accounting Standards Board (IASB) and International Standards on Auditing (IASs) are issued by the International Auditing and Assurance Standards Board (IAASB).

■ **changes in ethical codes**. Professional Bodies in the UK base their ethical codes on the IFAC code of ethics. This will be updated from time to time by IFAC, which may then result in updates to the code of ethics of the professional accounting bodies.

■ **changes in tax and companies legislation**. Taxation legislation is issued by the Government with amendments to the tax legislation and rates made in the annual Budget. Companies' legislation is through The Companies Act (2006).

■ **changes in relevant criminal law including bribery, fraud, money laundering**. Changes, amendments and updates to criminal legislation are contained within statute law. For more details on bribery see page 47; fraud is covered in more detail on page 46 and money laundering is covered in Chapter 6.

■ **any additional changes in regulation of accounting, reporting, tax compliance, audit and the accounting and finance profession**. In addition to specific changes in accounting standards, codes of ethics and various relevant legislation professional accountants must keep up-to-date with any additional changes to areas relating to the work that they carry out.

keeping up-to-date

There are three main ways in which a professional accountant can keep up-to-date with technical changes. These are:

■ reading professional journals

■ enrolling on updating courses

■ complying with continuing professional development (CPD) requirements for qualified professional accountants.

professional journals

The professional accountancy bodies in the UK publish their own magazines (professional journals). These magazines provide excellent updates on current accounting practice, taxation and auditing and are a good way for professional accountants to keep their knowledge up-to-date. Many of these journals also have websites that give further detail on articles included in the magazines, together with links to sites which provide more detailed information. Some examples of journals produced by professional accounting bodies are listed below together with the accounting body that it relates to.

■ Accounting and Business – ACCA

■ Economia – ICAEW

■ Financial Management – CIMA

■ Public Finance – CIPFA

■ Accounting Technician – AAT

In addition to these journals there are other accountancy related magazines including 'Accountancy Magazine', 'Accountancy Age' and 'Part-Qualified (PQ)' magazine all of which provided up-to-date technical articles which will help professional accountants to maintain their technical knowledge.

updating courses

The professional accounting bodies expect their members to maintain current accounting, taxation and auditing knowledge. As these professional bodies have access to a wide range of expertise within their membership they will regularly run specialist courses for members to attend which will update them on the latest accounting and finance information. Although the professional bodies will usually charge their members for these courses they will normally be reasonable priced for the content provided.

Many of the large accounting firms also run regular updating courses for their staff. With large numbers of professional staff they will have specialist technical departments that produce detailed briefings on accounting and finance matters. They will also run regular training courses for both student employees and qualified technical staff.

continuing professional development

Professional accounting bodies expect their members to maintain professional competence through **continuing professional development (CPD)**. This is learning that accountants need to carry out to stay competent. Each professional accounting body recommends that its members should follow a programme of relevant continuing professional development (CPD) each year. CPD is generally measured by the outcomes and benefits the members get from doing CPD.

CPD PROCESS

We will look at two accounting bodies, the Institute of Chartered Accountants in England and Wales (ICAEW) and the Association of Accounting Technicians (AAT) as examples of how the CPD process works for a professional accountant.

ICAEW process

ICAEW requires its members to maintain and develop their skills throughout their career. Its members must confirm that they are doing this by making a CPD declaration every year. ICAEW do not dictate how much CPD its members should do either in terms of time or by a points system. Instead the ICAEW says that its members must complete as much development activity as they feel they need to remain competent in their role.

ICAEW members are expected to take the Reflect, Act, Impact, Declare approach. This is explained by ICAEW as follows:

- **reflect**, consider your development needs and how you can meet them, and create a plan of action
- **act**, carry out your chosen CPD activity
- **impact**, evaluate the effectiveness of what you have done. Are you satisfied that your actions have enabled you to meet your objectives, or do you need more work in this area?
- **declare**, each year you must declare your compliance by making a CPD declaration between 1 November and 31 January

As the AAT is the accounting body that you are currently studying with we will look at the AAT CPD cycle in more detail. You will notice there are a number of similarities with the ICAEW policy.

AAT CPD cycle

The AAT CPD policy requires its members to undertake sufficient CPD to ensure their competence to carry out the roles that they carry out. Part of this requirement is to go through the CPD cycle at least once in a 12 month period, or twice for members in practice. The CPD cycle consists of four stages:

- assess
- plan
- action
- evaluate

We will now look briefly at what is involved at each stage.

assess

In this step of the CPD cycle the member should start by asking the following questions:

- what are my CPD goals?
- what must I learn to achieve my goals?
- what can I do well and where could I improve?
- are there any particular gaps in my skill set that I can prioritise?

By answering these questions the member will identify the areas which he/she needs to focus on for professional development.

plan

Once the member has identified the areas he/she needs to develop it is time to work out how to fill this gap in his/her skills. The AAT have an extensive CPD zone on their website, https://www.aat.org.uk/myaat/cpd_zone/, which includes a 'CPD planner template' that members can use to plan out the continuing professional development that they are going to undertake. At this stage the questions to ask are:

- what do I need to do to meet my goals?
- how does this fit with the resources I have available, in terms of time and money?
- what kind of learning do I respond to best?
- do I prefer on-the-job training, attending courses or e-learning?

By answering these questions members can decide what type of development they can afford to undertake in terms of the cost and the time that they can dedicate to it. They can then arrange the necessary training to undertake.

action

At this point in the CPD cycle the member can stop asking themselves questions and actually 'take action'. In simple terms this means carry out the plan. This may be through attending training courses, obtaining on-the-job training from experienced colleagues, self study, research etc. A full list of possible CPD activities is detailed at the end of this section.

Because the AAT expect its members to record the CPD that they achieve it is useful to write down anything new that has been learned. This will make it much easier to fill in the CPD records that need to be sent to the AAT. As a member you do not have to limit the CPD that you record to formal training courses, you can also include informal learning which has helped you to do your job more effectively.

evaluate

Once the CPD activity has been carried out by the member he/she must evaluate whether it has been worthwhile and assess the benefits that he/she has gained.

Evaluation can be seen in two parts. Firstly on a basic level was the activity worth the time and money that the member spent on it? Secondly, the member needs to reflect on how the CPD fits into his/her overall development and whether it means that he/she can carry out his/her work more effectively.

At this stage the final set of questions that need to be asked are:

■ how useful has my learning been?

■ do I feel better equipped for my current role as a result?

■ have I achieved the goals I set myself?

■ are there any goals that remain which can be carried forward to my next CPD plan?

Going through this cycle twice a year will focus a member of the AAT on what development needs he/she has and how best to achieve them. By maintaining effective CPD this will also ensure that the professional competence of the member will be maintained together with an ethical approach to his/her work.

The following are specific examples of appropriate CPD that have been identified by the AAT, however any learning, training or experience that helps you do your job or develop your career counts as CPD.

■ workshops, training courses, conferences

■ AAT or other professional body branch/society meetings

■ planned coaching from colleagues or specialists

■ structured discussion groups

■ studying for further qualifications

■ online/CD-Rom courses

■ planned reading/research

■ using audio, video or IT resources

■ special project work or job secondment

■ hands-on development of skills (eg IT or presentations)

■ membership of local or professional groups

■ voluntary work

With all the choices above, it would seem very straightforward for an accountant to achieve the required amount of CPD. However, it is very important to stress that the CPD that is undertaken by the accountant must be relevant, and significant learning must take place. For example, attending a local AAT meeting is only relevant CPD if the subjects discussed are relevant to the accountant's job. Similarly, acting voluntarily as treasurer for a local cricket club may be relevant 'voluntary' CPD but working on a Saturday morning as a dog walker at the local dog shelter may not be!

monitoring of CPD by the AAT

AAT members must keep CPD records which could be requested at any time by the AAT. Registered members of the AAT should expect their CPD to be monitored frequently by the AAT. CPD is a vital part of the regulation of members in practice and helps to reassure the public that the member maintains the necessary skills to fulfil his/her role effectively and professionally. Registered members in practice will be asked to submit their CPD records when they renew their registration on the members in practice scheme. Licensed members in practice or members doing voluntary work will be asked to submit their CPD records if they are selected at one of the AAT's CPD monitoring sessions which take place every February and September.

An AAT member who is subject to a disciplinary investigation will also be asked to submit his/her CPD records to the AAT.

CPD summary

The CPD process for ICAEW and AAT have been used as examples however, all professional accounting bodies have their own CPD policies which will follow a similar process and which will require its members to carry out appropriate continuing professional development to maintain up-to-date knowledge of changes to codes of practice, regulation and legislation affecting the accounting and finance sector.

WORKING WITHIN YOUR OWN CAPABILITIES

We have identified in the previous section that professional accountants must ensure that they maintain their professional competence. However, the range of work carried out by accountants in practice consists of a number of complex areas. It is therefore impossible for professional accountants to be experts in everything. Accountants must ensure that they work within the confines of their own professional experience, knowledge and expertise and of the client engagement that they are working on.

Firms of accountants should ensure that the staff they allocate to specific assignments have the appropriate knowledge and skills to carry out the work that is required of them with the necessary professional and technical competence. Where staff allocated to an assignment do not have the necessary levels of skills, expertise and experience, more senior members of staff must ensure that they are given appropriate supervision and guidance. They must also ensure that all work carried out by more junior, inexperienced members of staff is adequately reviewed.

A professional accountant who works outside the limits of his/her professional experience, knowledge and expertise will not be adhering to the fundamental ethical principle of professional competence and due care. If an accountant takes on a role or assignment knowing he/she does not have the necessary skills they would also be breaching the fundamental principles of integrity and professional behaviour.

REQUEST TO WORK BEYOND THE EMPLOYEE'S COMPETENCE

In this chapter we have identified the need for a professional accountant to ensure that he/she stays up-to-date with technical knowledge to ensure he/she is professionally competent. We have also looked at the need for an accountant to work within the limits of his/her capabilities. But what should a professional accountant do if they are asked by their employer to complete work for which they are not competent to carry out?

The easy answer would be to say 'don't do it!' or 'say no!' But when an accountant is employed in a professional practice or in business it is not always that easy. Management will expect their staff to carry out the work that they are given and the accountant will feel pressurised to complete the tasks that they are given to do.

The fundamental principle of professional competence and due care requires that a professional accountant only undertake tasks for which he/she has, or can obtain, sufficient specific training or experience. In addition to this a professional accountant in business should not intentionally mislead an employer as to the level of expertise or experience possessed, nor shall a professional accountant in business fail to seek appropriate expert advice and assistance when required.

There are a number of circumstances that will threaten the ability of an accountant in practice or in business to carry out work with the appropriate level of competence and due care. These include:

- if the accountant has insufficient time for properly performing or completing the relevant duties
- if the accountant has incomplete or inadequate information for carrying out the work properly
- if the accountant has insufficient experience, training and/or education

- if there are inadequate resources for example time, for the work to be carried out properly

The significance of these threats will depend on the level of supervision and review that the accountant is getting at work. However, these threats must not be ignored and if the accountant decides that they are not insignificant then steps must be taken to reduce the threats to an acceptable level or to actually eliminate them completely.

Safeguards that may be considered by the accountant to reduce or eliminate threats include:

- obtaining additional advice or training
- ensuring that there is adequate time available for performing the relevant duties
- obtaining assistance from someone with the necessary expertise
- where appropriate consulting with a more senior member of staff, usually a manager at work, independent experts or a relevant professional body

If even after doing this the threats cannot be eliminated or reduced to an acceptable level the accountant should consider whether to refuse to do the work. If the accountant does decide to refuse he/she should clearly tell the appropriate people, stating his/her reasons for refusing.

We will now look at an example of a situation where a professional accountant is asked to work beyond his competence and what he should do in this situation.

example

do you have the right expertise?

Ernie is an accountant who has been employed by Wrexisty Ltd for six months working in their Finance Department. His manager, Cyrus, has sent him an email asking him to complete the VAT Return for Wrexisty Ltd which includes some complex imports and exports. Cyrus has also told Ernie that he will be away on a business trip for the next four days and the VAT Return must be submitted before the deadline, which is in three days. Ernie has not previously completed a VAT Return for the business and the last time he studied VAT was when he completed his accounting qualification. He also has his own month-end duties to complete that will take up all his time in the next three days.

What should Ernie do in this situation?

Cyrus has requested Ernie to carry out work that is beyond his professional experience, expertise and competence. This means that Ernie's fundamental ethical principle of professional competence and due care is being threatened. This threat is significant as Ernie will have no direct supervision from Cyrus if he carries out this work.

- First of all Ernie should speak to another member of staff in the department, explain the situation and ask their advice.

- He should also speak to someone more senior in the department to find out whether the VAT Return can take priority over his month-end duties.

- If he is still expected to complete the VAT Return he should obtain assistance from someone else with the necessary expertise, this could be another member of staff or alternatively the company's auditors.

If after trying all these options Ernie still feels he does not have the necessary expertise to complete the VAT Return he should raise the issue with someone more senior in the company, explaining why he is unable to carry out the work that he has been asked to do.

Ernie should not try and complete the VAT Return without the necessary expertise.

It is clear that accountants are expected to take advice, or ask for assistance or training if they do not have the necessary skills to carry out an assignment or task that they have been asked to complete.

The accountant should also not intentionally mislead an employer as to the level of expertise or experience he/she has, nor should an accountant in business fail to seek appropriate expert advice and assistance when required. We will now explore what this means in more detail.

Many employees are ambitious and keen to progress within the organisation for which they work. Therefore, when there is an opportunity to do some more challenging work, this can be seen by employees as a way to show their ability and make a name for themselves. In this situation there can sometimes be a temptation for an employee to 'talk up' his/her experience and ability to perform the work in question in order to persuade the employer that he/she is the 'right person for the job'.

In the case of members of the accounting profession it is important that they should not exaggerate their own expertise or experience in relation to accounting skills. If an employed professional accountant tells his/her employer that they have the necessary skills and expertise to carry out a particular task when they do not, this can have much more serious consequences.

This point is illustrated in the following example.

example

a question of experience

When Amit Odedra joined the Accounts Department of Warwick & Parks six months ago, he made it clear at his interview that he was very ambitious and keen to progress within the company. Mike Smith, the Finance Director, has noticed that Amit is very hard working and is regularly the last person to leave the office. He has therefore asked Amit to take on responsibility for preparing the monthly payroll for the company.

Amit has never done any payroll work before but would really like to take on the additional responsibility. What should Amit do in this situation?

Amit is very keen to progress within Warwick & Parks, but as an accountant he should be aware that ethically he must not mislead his employer about the extent of his expertise and experience. Consequently, he should explain to Mike that whilst he is keen to take on the extra responsibility, he has no previous experience in payroll and so would need some training in this area before he could perform the additional work.

If Amit did not make Mike aware of this and took on the additional responsibility of payroll without any training, the implications for Warwick & Parks could be very serious. Firstly, it is likely that the payroll would be incorrectly prepared which could mean (if the error was not picked up) that staff were paid the wrong amounts. Secondly, calculations of Pay As You Earn (PAYE) and National Insurance (NI) for payment to the Her Majesty's Revenue & Customs (HMRC) could be incorrect which could ultimately result in the company being fined.

We can see from this example that the fundamental principle of professional competence and due care is very relevant to the employed accountant. It would be ethically wrong for a professional accountant to mislead the employer as to his/her expertise and experience. Errors could result which would have serious consequences for the employer.

PROFESSIONAL LIABILITY

In addition to breaching his/her fundamental ethical principles, a professional accountant who acts beyond his/her professional experience, knowledge and experience may be liable to his/her client.

a definition of liability

Liability means **'having legal responsibility for something with the possibility of having to pay damages'.**

Liability can arise from a number of causes, including criminal acts, breach of contract in the supply of services, breach of trust, professional negligence and fraud.

In law **negligence** is a breach of a duty of care that is implied in a particular situation or relationship. For example, a railway company has a duty of care for the safe transit of its passengers and an accountant has a duty of care to carry out assignments in a skilled and professional manner. If the railway company fails to observe safety measures (such as red signals) and the accountant makes mistakes in a tax return, in different ways they are both held to be negligent. We will now look at liability for professional negligence on the part of a member of the accounting profession. **Professional negligence** may occur if a client, to whom the accountant owes a duty to exercise reasonable care and skill, suffers a financial loss that can be proved is the fault of the accountant. Additionally, the accountant will have entered into a contract with the client, so this may be a breach of contract and in certain cases there may even be accusations of fraud.

We will now look at an example of professional negligence and breach of contract.

example

Cecil is a professional accountant who works as a sole practitioner. Earlier in the year he prepared the tax return for his client, Amos, which included income that Amos has earned from some complex share transactions. HMRC have now investigated Amos's tax affairs in relation to this return and have found that the tax calculations are incorrect and that Amos has underpaid a substantial amount of tax. They have fined Amos for this error and have sent him a demand for the underpaid tax.

In this situation what can Amos do?

If Amos can prove that Cecil has not exercised reasonable care and skill and that he has suffered financial loss he can sue Cecil for professional negligence. As Amos also has a contract with Cecil to complete his tax return he could also sue for breach of contract.

minimising the risk of professional negligence

For all assignments the following points should be covered to ensure that the possibility of a client suing an accountant for professional negligence is minimised:

■ an accountant should ensure that before taking on an assignment the exact duties to be included (and equally as important, excluded) in the assignment are written down and agreed by both the accountant and the client. This would normally be done in the letter of engagement

■ if further duties are added to an assignment then the accountant should ensure that these are also written down and agreed by both parties

■ where an accountant gives a client advice without having been provided with all the information he/she needs, the accountant must make sure that the client is aware of any limitations to this advice and that this is written down

■ if the accountant prepares unaudited accounts or financial statements for a client he/she must clearly mark on the documents that they are confidential and solely for the private use of the client

■ if an assignment is very complex an accountant should take specialist advice or suggest that the client does so

professional indemnity insurance

All accountants hope that they will never be put in the position where a client brings a legal case against them for professional negligence. However, it is possible that at some time this may happen. Accountants in practice should ensure that they have adequate **professional indemnity insurance**. This type of insurance is taken out by an accountant (or other professional) as cover against legal liability to compensate a third party (normally a client) who has sustained injury, loss or damage through a breach in the accountant's duty of care. (**Note**: professional indemnity insurance is strongly recommended for student accountants who undertake self-employed work.)

We will now look at an example where the issue of professional liability could arise.

example

a question of professional liability

Christopher Matthews works as an accountant in practice. He has recently received a request from the Managing Director of one of his clients to provide him with some personal advice on inheritance tax. Christopher has no experience in this area of taxation and has never given advice on inheritance tax before.

Christopher is considering reading up on this area of tax and taking on this assignment. However, he thinks it would be a good idea to make sure his professional indemnity insurance is up-to-date.

Is this appropriate professional and ethical behaviour on Christopher's part?

If Christopher is unsure of his expertise regarding inheritance tax he should ensure that he gets the necessary advice and guidance from an appropriately qualified person. He should only take on the assignment if he considers that he has the professional and technical competence to carry out the work satisfactorily.

It would be unprofessional for Christopher to rely on his professional indemnity insurance to cover the risk that he may not carry out the work properly. It is also unlikely that a court would allow him to rely on this should the client bring a legal action for damages against him were his advice to result in the client losing money.

All accountants should have professional indemnity insurance. But this should not be used as a 'safety net' in situations where an accountant does not have the necessary skills to carry out an assignment.

Chapter Summary

■ Professional accountants should ensure that they have the necessary competence to carry out any work that they are allocated.

■ By qualifying with a professional accounting body a professional accountant will have trained and studied to attain professional competence.

■ Accountants are required to maintain their professional competence and to keep up-to-date with new developments in the accounting profession.

■ Critical areas where accountants must maintain their professional competence are:

– changes in financial reporting and auditing standards

– changes in ethical codes

– changes in tax and companies legislation

– changes in relevant criminal law including bribery, fraud and money laundering

– any additional changes in regulation of accounting, reporting, tax compliance, audit, and the accounting and finance profession

■ Accountants should keep up-to-date by reading professional journals, enrolling on updating courses and carrying out continuing professional development (CPD).

■ Professional accountants must ensure that they work within their own capabilities.

■ If an accountant is asked to carry out work that is beyond his/her capabilities he/she should obtain additional advice or training, ensure there is adequate time to complete the work, obtain assistance from someone with the necessary expertise and, where appropriate, consult with more senior staff, an independent expert or a relevant professional body.

■ If an accountant is negligent in his/her duties he could be liable ie legally responsible with the possibility of having to pay damages. This could be for a criminal act such as fraud or money laundering, breach of contract, breach of trust or professional negligence.

■ Members of the accounting profession should have sufficient professional indemnity insurance to cover against legal liability to compensate a client or third party that has sustained loss through a breach of the accountant's duty of care.

**Key
Terms**

professional competence   the necessary skills and expertise to carry out existing and new work to the required professional standard

professional journals   magazines published by the professional accounting bodies in the UK which include up-to-date information on current accounting practice

continuing professional development (CPD)   the way in which accountants maintain their knowledge and skills to ensure that they remain professionally competent

professional negligence   this may occur where a client, to whom an accountant owes a duty of care, suffers a financial loss that can be proved to be the fault of the accountant

professional indemnity insurance   insurance that an accountant takes out to cover any damages he/she may have to pay a client due to professional negligence

Activities

4.1 Give two different ways in which a professional accountant can keep up-to-date with technical changes.

1	
2	

4.2 Erica is a professional accountant with her own practice. She has a large number of small clients for whom she prepares tax returns, completes their VAT Returns and draws up their accounts.

Given her client profile, state one critical area of technical knowledge in which Erica must keep up-to-date and explain your reasons for this.

4.3 Portas & Wright is a large firm of accountants in Moorbridge. Its main business is preparing financial statements and providing external audit services for some of its clients.

Given its client profile, state two critical areas of technical knowledge on which Portas & Wright should run regular training courses. Explain your reasons for this.

4.4 All professional accounting bodies require their members to undertake continuing professional development (CPD). State the main fundamental ethical principle that is safeguarded by CPD.

4.5 Helmut is a recently qualified professional accountant in business working for Freemantle Ltd. He has been asked by his manager to prepare some complex depreciation calculations on some properties owned by the business which have recently been revalued. He has not carried out work like this before.

State two safeguards that Helmut should consider to reduce the threats to his fundamental ethical principle of professional competence and due care.

4.6 Edwin has recently been employed by Frederickson & Brewer, a medium sized firm of accountants. On his curriculum vitae (CV) Edwin stated that he has experience in completing VAT Returns when in fact he has only ever completed a VAT Return in professional accounting examinations. Edwin is asked to take responsibility for completing the quarterly VAT Return for one of Frederickson & Brewer's larger clients.

What should Edwin do in these circumstances?

4.7 Michaela, a professional accountant in practice, has provided taxation advice to her client, Nigel. Michaela did not have the necessary technical expertise to provide this advice and Nigel has ended up incurring a fine from HMRC.

If it is proved that Michaela has acted outside her professional competence, on what grounds may Nigel be able to sue Michaela for compensation?

State two grounds.

1	
2	

4.8 What type of insurance should professional accountants have to cover them against legal liability to compensate a client who has sustained financial loss through a breach of the accountant's duty of care?

5 Confidentiality

this chapter covers...

This chapter looks in more detail at the principle of confidentiality in relation to professional ethics.

Specific areas covered include:

- *the accountant's duty of confidentiality in relation to the client's or employer's affairs*

- *the circumstances where confidential information can be disclosed*

- *the Data Protection Act and the way in which it affects members of the accounting profession*

CONFIDENTIALITY

duty of confidentiality

One of the principles of professional ethics that we introduced in Chapter 1 is **confidentiality**. This means that information obtained during the course of an accountant's professional work should not be disclosed without proper and specific authority or unless there is a legal duty to do so. As this is such a fundamental principle of professional ethics, we will now look at this in more detail.

Members of the accounting profession have a 'duty of confidentiality' which means that they have **an obligation to respect the confidentiality of information about a client's or employer's affairs which has been gained during their employment or during the course of their professional work**. In addition to ensuring that they themselves observe this duty of confidentiality accountants must also make sure that any staff they supervise or manage also respect the principle of confidentiality.

We now give an example of a situation where an accountant must observe his/her duty of confidentiality.

example

a duty of confidentiality

Elliot Graves has been employed in the Accounts Department of Simons & Simons for a number of years and currently works as the Financial Accountant for the firm. On the train home from work on Friday evening he meets a friend and they start chatting. The conversation moves on to work and his friend asks Elliot how the job is going. He then goes on to ask how Simons & Simons are doing and specifically asks what kind of a financial year the company has had.

How should Elliot answer his friend's questions?

Elliot has a duty of confidentiality to his employers not to disclose any confidential information about the company that he works for. Elliot can answer his friend's first question as to whether his job is going well as this is a personal enquiry about Elliot himself. However, Elliot should explain to his friend that it is not appropriate for him to discuss confidential information about Simons & Simons financial results.

using confidential information

In addition to ensuring that they do not disclose confidential information, professional accountants must ensure that they do not use, or appear to use, any information that they have access to for their own personal advantage or for the advantage of a third party, eg colleague, friend or family member.

We will now look in more detail at what this actually means. The point is illustrated in the following example.

---

example

a question of advice

Lubna Mirza is employed by a small firm of accountants and has been working on the year-end accounts of one of their largest clients, Richards Ltd. During the time that she spends at the client's premises Lubna learns that the company is currently in talks to take over another local company which is owned by a close friend of hers. The owner of Richards Ltd, James Richards, has mentioned that he would be willing to pay up to £250,000 for the firm, but only initially intends to offer £200,000.

Should Lubna tell her friend about James Richards' intentions? If not, would it be acceptable for her to give her friend advice about what offer to accept for her business?

Lubna has a duty of confidentiality to the client and so should not disclose any information she has obtained about Richards Ltd without specific authority from the company or unless she is legally obliged to do so. If she were to give her friend advice about what offer to accept, based on the information that she now knows, she would be using information that she had gained to benefit her friend (a third party), which is not acceptable.

Therefore, if Lubna's friend asks her for advice she should explain that Richards Ltd is one of her firm's clients and should suggest that the friend obtains independent specialist advice on how to value her business.

This example shows that an accountant must not use information for his/her personal advantage or for that of a third party.

We will now look at the second point regarding the use of confidential information. This is that accountants must not **appear** to use information that they have gained for their own personal advantage or that of a third party.

The point here is that even if the accountant is confident that he/she has not used confidential information for his/her own personal benefit or that of another, the accountant must also ensure that there is no possibility of anyone **thinking** that they have. It should not **appear** that the accountant has used confidential information inappropriately.

This is best illustrated with an example, using the same scenario as the last example.

---

example

the danger of 'appearing' to pass on confidential information

We will now return to the example of Lubna Mirza that we looked at above. If Lubna follows the course of action recommended in the example she can be confident that she has not used confidential information about Richards Ltd to benefit her friend.

Suppose that James Richards has completed the takeover of Lubna's friend's business and has paid £230,000 for it. If he were then to find out that the owner of the business he had bought was a close personal friend of Lubna's, he could quite legitimately question whether Lubna had passed on the information to her friend about what his maximum offer would be.

What could Lubna do/have done to ensure that her duty of confidentiality was not called into question?

As soon as she knew that James was intending to make an offer to buy her friend's business Lubna should have informed James of her relationship with the owner. She should also have explained to him that she is fully aware of her duty of confidentiality regarding information that she gains about a client and will not pass on any information. This would get her out of the dangerous situation where she could have 'appeared' to have advised the owner – simply because James would not have known otherwise.

the ongoing duty of confidentiality

We have already established that an accountant has an obligation to respect the confidentiality of information about employers or clients during the time that he/she is employed or is working for the client. This duty of confidentiality extends to the period **after the relationship has ended**.

In practice this means that any information that the accountant gains in the course of the professional work he/she carries out for a client remains confidential – even after the accountant is no longer employed by the client.

Similarly, information regarding an accountant's employer remains confidential even when the accountant moves to another employer.

DISCLOSURE OF CONFIDENTIAL INFORMATION

Having established that accountants have a duty of confidentiality, we will now look at the circumstances where confidential information can be disclosed. There are three main situations where it is acceptable to disclose confidential information. These are shown in the diagram below.

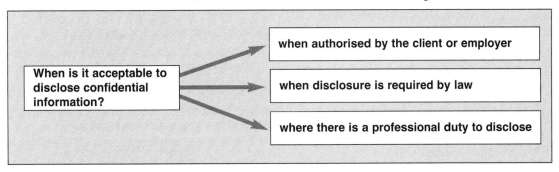

We will now look in more detail at these three situations.

authorised disclosure

In certain circumstances, the client or employer may actually ask the accountant to disclose information that would otherwise have been treated as confidential.

The example that follows highlights a common situation where a client authorises the accountant to disclose confidential information to a third party.

example

authority to disclose

You work for a firm of accountants and receive a telephone call from a local builders' merchants asking for financial information about one of your clients who has requested to trade with them on credit.

How should you deal with this call?

Financial information regarding your client is confidential. Therefore you should not disclose any information about your client to the builders' merchants unless you have been authorised by the client to do so. You should contact your client to explain the situation and obtain specific authority to provide the financial information to the caller. Although verbal authority is acceptable, it would be better if this authority was given in writing.

When authority to disclose has been obtained from the client you can give the requested information to the builders' merchants. When doing this it is important to include a disclaimer making it clear that this is for the use of the builders' merchants only and is given purely to help them to make a decision about whether or not to supply goods on credit to your client. You should also explain that the information is given without any financial responsibility on the part of yourself or the firm for which you work.

This example illustrates that where a client has given permission, the accountant is then able to disclose confidential information. The main point here is that the accountant must get specific authority from the client before doing so.

disclosure required by law

In some circumstances the accountant will be faced with a legal requirement to disclose confidential information. This legal requirement to disclose confidential information can be divided into two main categories:

■ where the information is required as evidence in a court of law

■ where the law requires that information must be revealed to the relevant authorities in situations where the law has been broken

This is illustrated in the diagram below.

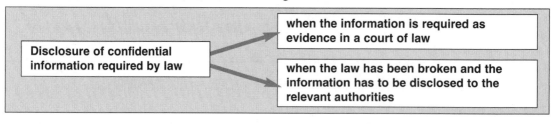

We will now look at each of these two requirements in more detail.

evidence in court

There may be circumstances where an accountant is required to provide evidence in a legal case in court. The accountant may receive a witness summons from the court and be required to:

■ provide documents which will be used in court as evidence, and/or

■ to appear in court in person to give evidence

Alternatively the accountant might be the subject of a court order requiring him/her to disclose confidential information about the client.

In any of these circumstances the accountant has a legal obligation to comply with the request. As a consequence the accountant must break his/her duty of confidentiality to the client or employer, even if the client or employer has refused to give permission for the evidence to be provided. The power of the law, through the witness summons or court order, is stronger and will prevail here.

The following example illustrates this point in practice.

example

a legal question of confidentiality

Rachael Thomas acts as the accountant for Rolls Ltd. One of Rolls Ltd's suppliers has taken them to court for failure to pay for goods that have been supplied to them. There has been an ongoing dispute between Rolls and this supplier which has resulted in the non-payment by Rolls.

Rachael has been asked to provide copies of all documents relevant to this dispute, including invoices and correspondence, as evidence in the case. She has also been told that she may be required to appear in court as a witness to give evidence.

In these circumstances what steps should Rachael take before providing this information?

The information that Rachael has been asked to provide to the court is confidential. The first thing that she should do is to make her client, Rolls Ltd, aware that she expects to be called as a witness thereby giving them the opportunity to give her authority to provide the information in court. If they agree then she is free to provide the relevant documents or evidence as requested.

If, despite being informed of Rachael's likely appearance in court, Rolls Ltd refuses to give authority for her to disclose then Rachael must wait until she receives a witness summons. When this occurs she is legally required to comply with the summons and provide the relevant documentation, and if necessary, appear in court herself to give evidence.

disclosure where infringement of the law has occurred

Where a client or an employer has broken the law there may be a requirement for the accountant to disclose information to the relevant authorities that would otherwise be considered confidential.

A good example of this is in relation to money laundering.

A definition of money laundering is:

'to move illegally acquired cash through financial systems so that it appears to be legally acquired.'

Basically, as the name 'money laundering' suggests, when the money has been gained through illegal activities it is seen as 'dirty money'. By using that money in legitimate trade or investment activities this is like 'washing' or 'laundering' the money so that it then appears to be 'clean' and legally obtained.

The current legislation relating to money laundering is the **Proceeds of Crime Act 2002,** the **Terrorism Act 2000,** and the **Money Laundering Regulations 2007**. It requires accountants to report immediately any suspicion that they have that money has been gained from illegal activities to the National Crime Agency (NCA).

Money laundering is covered in detail in Chapter 6. It is clear that in the circumstances described here the accountant has to disclose confidential information about a client if he/she considers that the client has broken the law. Disclosure in these circumstances should be made to the Money Laundering Reporting Office (MLRO) at the accountant's firm or to NCA.

Accountants may also be permitted to disclose confidential information if he/she suspects an employer, colleague or client has committed, or may commit, an act which is illegal or unethical. This will be covered in more detail when we look at internal whistle-blowing in Chapter 6.

a professional duty to disclose

In certain circumstances, an accountant may have a **professional duty** to disclose confidential information. These circumstances are summarised below:

- to comply with the quality review of an IFAC (International Federation of Accountants) member body or other relevant professional body

- to respond to an inquiry by the professional accounting body or by a regulatory body of an ethical, investigatory or disciplinary nature

- to protect the professional interests of the accountant in legal proceedings

- to comply with technical standards and ethical requirements

We will now look briefly at each of these four points. Taking the first point, if a member body of IFAC such as the ICAEW decides to carry out a quality review then the accountant is obliged to disclose confidential information to help with the review. Other member bodies of IFAC include ACCA, CIPFA and CIMA.

In the second point, a professional accountant must disclose confidential information if it is in response **to an inquiry by the professional accounting body or by a regulatory body of an ethical, investigatory or disciplinary nature**. This inquiry could be in relation to the actions of the accountant in question, or an inquiry relating to an investigation into the actions of another accountant. If the accountant finds that in order to respond to the inquiry from his/her professional accounting body he/she must disclose information that would otherwise have been seen as confidential, he/she has a professional duty to disclose this.

This type of situation could arise where the professional accounting body has received a complaint from a client of one of its members regarding the fee that they have been charged for accounting work that the member has carried out. The accounting body has a duty to investigate this complaint. In order to answer the questions that it raises with him/her the accountant may have to disclose confidential client information relating to the work that he/she has carried out.

Thirdly, an accountant has a professional duty to disclose if he/she is to protect his/her professional interests in legal proceedings. If, for example, an accountant was faced with legal action against him/her by a client, he/she would be permitted to disclose otherwise confidential information to protect his/her professional good name.

In the fourth point, an accountant has a professional duty to disclose confidential information in order **to comply with technical standards and ethical requirements**. Technical standards in this case refer to International Financial Reporting Standards (IFRSs), International Accounting Standards (IASs) and other relevant standards. Ethical requirements are those set out in the accountants' Code of Professional Ethics.

Deciding whether to disclose confidential information where there is a professional duty to disclose is a particularly difficult and complex area. Accountants are, therefore, specifically advised to seek professional or legal advice before disclosing confidential information in these circumstances if they are in any doubt.

the decision to disclose

If an accountant makes the decision to disclose confidential information, there are three points which must be considered before making this disclosure. These points can be summarised as follows:

- the accountant must decide whether he/she knows all the facts regarding the issue and has enough evidence to back up these facts. If he/she does not have enough evidence then the accountant must use his/her professional judgement to decide to what extent (if any) the confidential information can be disclosed

- next, the accountant must decide who is the right person(s) to whom this information should be disclosed, and also how it should be communicated, for example by letter, report or verbally. This decision should ensure that the person provided with the information has the necessary authority to act upon it

- finally, the accountant must consider whether he/she would face any legal consequences from disclosing confidential information, and if so how serious these consequences could be

We can see that the accounting profession takes the subject of disclosure of confidential information very seriously and members must be very careful when deciding whether or not they should disclose.

In any circumstances where an accountant is unsure whether or not they should disclose confidential information, or where they are unclear as to how much they should disclose, they should consider taking legal advice from a solicitor or contact his/her accounting body's Advice Line. It is always better to get a second opinion if there is any doubt over the action that should be taken, rather than risk making the wrong decision.

DATA PROTECTION ACT

When an accountant in practice works for a client he/she will have access to a huge amount of information about the client. As we have discussed above, the accountant has a duty of confidentiality to the client regarding the disclosure of this information. In addition to this there are legal requirements set out in the Data Protection Act 1998.

The **Data Protection Act** gives individuals the right to know what information is held about them. It provides a framework to ensure that personal information is handled properly.

The Act works in two ways. Firstly, it states that anyone who processes personal information must comply with eight principles, which make sure that personal information is:

- fairly and lawfully processed
- processed for limited purposes
- adequate, relevant and not excessive
- accurate and up-to-date
- not kept for longer than is necessary
- processed in line with the individual's rights
- secure
- not transferred to other countries without adequate protection

The second area covered by the Act provides individuals with important rights, including the right to find out what personal information is held on computer and paper records about them.

Enforcement of the requirements of the Data Protection Act is carried out by the **Information Commissioner's Office** (ICO). Should an individual or organisation feel they are being denied access to personal information that they are entitled to, or feel their information has not been handled according to the eight principles, they can contact the ICO. Complaints are usually dealt with informally, but if this is not possible, enforcement action can be taken. Action taken by the ICO can range from issuing a 'stop now' order, to prosecuting those who commit an offence under the Data Protection Act.

notification

There is a statutory requirement for every organisation that processes personal information to register with the ICO. It must reregister annually and pay an annual fee to the ICO to remain registered. **Notification** is the process by which the person controlling the data gives the ICO details about the way in which the company processes data. Failure to notify the ICO could result in a fine if convicted. The next example illustrates this point.

example

Sonya is a professional accountant who owns and runs a small accountancy practice with 12 employees. She has failed to notify the Information Commissioner of the way in which the practice processes data.

Sonya has committed a criminal offence under the Data Protection Act and consequently could be fined if convicted.

■ Accountants have an obligation to respect the confidentiality of information about a client's or employer's affairs acquired in the course of professional work.

■ Accountants must ensure that any staff who work for them also follow the principle of confidentiality.

■ Confidential information should not be used or appear to be used for the personal advantage of the member or a third party.

■ The duty of confidentiality continues after the end of the relationship between the accountant and the employer or client.

■ Confidential information can be disclosed when a client or employer authorises the disclosure.

■ If the law specifically requires it confidential information about a client or employer can be disclosed.

■ If an accountant has a professional duty to either comply with accounting standards, protect his/her professional interests in legal proceedings or respond to an inquiry by his/her professional body, confidential information may be disclosed.

■ If an accountant requires advice on detailed ethical issues he/she should contact his/her professional accounting body's Ethics Advice Line.

■ The Data Protection Act provides a framework to ensure personal information is handled properly.

■ The person in an organisation that controls information has a duty to notify the Information Commissioner's Office of the organisation's process for handling data.

Key Terms

duty of confidentiality	the accountant's obligation to respect confidential information about the client or employer's affairs
ongoing duty of confidentiality	the fact that the accountant's duty of confidentiality continues even after the end of the relationship between the accountant and the employer or client
authorised disclosure of confidential information	disclosure of confidential information by an accountant following authorisation by the client or employer
disclosure required by law	the legal requirement for an accountant to disclose financial information about a client or an employer
money laundering	to move illegally acquired cash through financial systems so that it appears to be legally acquired
NCA	National Crime Agency
Data Protection Act	legislation to ensure that data held about individuals is handled properly
ICO	Information Commissioner's Office

Activities

5.1 The duty of confidentiality to a client on the part of a professional accountant is only applicable for the duration of the assignment.

Is this statement **true** or **false**?

5.2 Robert, an accountant in practice, has been asked by Zeena, one of his clients, to provide her with some financial information about another client who is one of Zeena's customers and who Zeena is currently in a legal dispute with.

Explain whether Robert can provide Zeena with any information about her client.

5.3 Findlay works for a firm of accountants in Moorbridge. He receives a letter from a local office supplies company asking for financial information about one of his clients who has requested credit terms with them. Findlay is aware that the information they have requested is confidential.

What should Findlay do in these circumstances?

5.4 Darren is a professional accountant who works as a sole practitioner. He suspects that one of his new clients, Jessica, has deliberately failed to declare all her income on her tax return from the previous year.

In these circumstances can Darren disclose confidential information about Jessica to the National Crime Agency?

5.5 An accountant has a professional duty to disclose confidential information to protect his/her

[   ] interests in [   ].

Select the appropriate words from the selection below to fill the gaps in the sentence above.

personal   **taxation affairs**   **professional**

organisation's   **financial matters**   **legal proceedings**

5.6   What is the name of the process by which the person in an organisation who controls data informs the Information Commissioner's Office (ICO) about the way in which the organisation handles data?

6 Codes of conduct and organisational values

this chapter covers...

This chapter first looks at business ethics and conducts of conduct and practice that businesses put in place, and the effect that the corporate culture and the 'tone at the top' in an organisation has on the ethical conduct of its staff.

It then covers the key ethical organisational values that should be included in a business's code of practice to ensure that it complies with the spirit of the regulations it must comply with.

The chapter will also look at the consequences of not complying with organisational values, codes of practice and regulations including the internal disciplinary procedures an accountant may face. It will also highlight the opportunity for an accountant to consider whistleblowing if he or she believes that an employer, colleague or client has acted illegally or unethically.

There is a detailed section looking at the money laundering offences and the professional accountant's duty to report money laundering.

The final section of the chapter looks at inappropriate client behaviour and how to deal with it and also the particular threats and safeguards an accountant faces to his/her fundamental ethical principles when dealing with clients.

BUSINESS ETHICS AND CODES OF CONDUCT AND PRACTICE

We have already introduced the ethical code in previous chapters for accountants and looked at how it is designed to guide accountants to behave ethically. It also sets out the required standards of professional behaviour that accountants should maintain and gives them guidance on how to achieve these standards. Each professional accounting body in the UK has based its own ethical code on that issued by IESBA and this consistent approach to professional ethics means that the public interest will be protected together with the reputation of the professional accounting bodies.

In addition to the guidance on professional ethics published by professional bodies, many organisations will have their own code of **business ethics.** These set out guidance on the conduct and values that govern decisions and actions within that individual organisation. This code is designed to help an individual in an organisation, faced with an ethical dilemma, to make the right choice between alternative courses of action. It also ensures that there is consistency in the conduct of all employees within the organisation.

The code of ethics for accountants prescribes a principle-based approach, ie identifying, evaluating and addressing threats to fundamental principles rather than a rules-based approach. Similarly, a principles-based approach should be adopted when applying a code of conduct or practice and these should be used as a guide rather than a set of rules.

Each company will include different elements which it considers are important in its code of business ethics. Examples of areas on which they may give guidance include:

- compliance with the law
- competing fairly
- how to act with integrity in all business dealings
- treating suppliers, partners and customers properly
- treating co-workers respectfully
- contributing to a healthy, safe and secure workplace
- respecting the environment and contributing to the community
- respecting human rights
- maintaining high standards of financial record-keeping and reporting

If you research business ethics, codes of conduct or codes of practice in your organisation you may well find a written policy that includes some of these points together with other areas relevant to your industry.

legal status of codes of conduct

Where a company introduces an ethical code of conduct this is not legally enforceable and criminal sanctions cannot be imposed on employees who do not comply with the code. However, there may be elements within the code that are based on laws, which could result in a criminal prosecution. For example, in the list above one of the points is 'contributing to a healthy, safe and secure workplace'. Although this could be included in a firm's code of conduct this is also regulated by the Health and Safety at Work Act.

the Institute of Business Ethics

The Institute of Business Ethics (IBE) was established in 1986 to encourage high standards of business behaviour based on ethical values. They raise public awareness of the importance of doing business ethically and collaborate with other UK and international organisations with interests and expertise in business ethics.

The IBE has produced a 'Simple ethical test for a business decision'. This test has three elements or questions to ask when faced with a business decision. These are:

- Transparency – do I mind others knowing what I have decided?
- Effect – who does my decision affect or hurt?
- Fairness – would my decision be considered fair by those affected?

By considering these three questions an individual within an organisation will consider the ethical implications of the decision he/she makes.

Members of the accounting profession must always behave ethically when working with others, whether it is clients, suppliers, colleagues or any other individual they come into contact with.

tone at the top

Tone at the top refers to the ethical atmosphere that is created in the workplace by the organisation's leadership. Management's attitude to ethics will have a trickle-down effect on the employees of the company. If the tone set by managers upholds ethical values and integrity, employees will be more inclined to uphold those same values. If, on the other hand, senior management appear unconcerned with acting ethically, employees will be more likely to feel that ethical conduct is not a focus within the organisation. Employees pay close attention to the behaviour and actions of their bosses, and they follow their lead.

The following example illustrates a situation where the tone at the top is important in an organisation.

example

Jonathan works for Excelsior limited, a company that supplies and fits curtains and blinds. During a sales team meeting the company's Sales Manager, Rebecca Grey presented her method for maximising sales revenue. She explained that when she visits customers she assesses how much money she thinks they have and changes the price that she will charge them accordingly. She also increases the price to certain customers so that she can offer them 'big discounts' and still make a profit. She encouraged all her team to do the same.

Rebecca's selling techniques are not ethical but as she is the boss she is setting the tone at the top within Excelsior and her sales team are likely to follow her lead and sell in the same unethical manner.

risk of unethical behaviour

The section above highlighted the risks that arise from the way in which a business operates. In addition to this there are risks that the organisation will face due to unethical behaviour on the part of its management and employees. The implementation of a strong code of conduct in the organisation and a positive corporate culture that encourages ethical behaviour from employees will help minimise the risks associated with unethical behaviour. However, accountants must be vigilant in their work to prevent and detect instances of unethical behaviour. The following example is an illustration of where an accountant could identify unethical behaviour in the workplace.

example

spotting unethical behaviour

Joe is an accountant working in the Accounts Payable Department of Webbey Ltd. As part of his responsibilities he processes the expense claims for all members of staff. He had just received two expense claims which he is concerned about. The first is from one of the salesmen. He has claimed for a 400 mile round trip to visit a client when Joe knows that the journey is less than 40 miles. The second is from the Finance Director who is claiming £575 for client entertainment for a round of golf and dinner at the local golf club. Joe knows that there were no clients involved in the golf day and it was the Finance Director and his three sons who were playing. Joe has now done some research and found that this is not the first time the Finance Director has claimed for a family event on his expenses, although in previous cases Joe has not been involved in processing the expense claim.

What are the issues for Joe and what should Joe do in these circumstances?

It is likely that in the case of the salesman it may be a genuine error with the salesman completing his expense claim incorrectly and claiming for 400 miles when he should have claimed for 40. Joe should point out the error to the salesman and ascertain whether this was a genuine mistake. He should then explain to the salesman the importance of being careful with expenses claims and the risk of being accused of unethical behaviour if he makes inaccurate claims.

The second situation is more difficult. In these circumstances Joe appears to have identified unethical behaviour on the part of the Finance Director. Due to his seniority in the organisation this puts Joe in a difficult position. Ideally in this case Joe should gather together all the information relating to the claim and present it to another director of the business explaining his concerns regarding the ethical dilemma he faces in processing the claims and the fact that the Finance Director is committing fraud. If the other director does not deal with the issue then Joe should consider taking advice from his professional accounting body as to what further action he should take.

reputational risk

Something that threatens the good name of a business or its reputation is known as a reputational risk. This can result from a number of different factors, the direct actions of the business, the actions of one or more of its employees, or the actions of a third party that is linked to the business such as a partner in a joint venture or a supplier. Damage to the reputation of a business can have a significant detrimental effect on the business causing loss of sales and profit, employees to resign and reluctance on the part of suppliers, customers and investors to be associated with the business.

A recent example of this is the damage to the reputation of the coffee chain Starbucks, which was hit by allegations of (legally) avoiding tax in the UK.

To avoid reputational risk damage, organisations must have good codes of conduct, strong governance and be transparent in its dealings with customers, suppliers, employees and all other external parties. In addition to this the organisation needs to be socially responsible and environmentally conscious.

ORGANISATIONAL AND PROFESSIONAL VALUES

Professional accountants are expected to comply with the law and with relevant regulations, however, organisations should also comply with 'the spirit' of the regulations, ie how these regulations are expected to work in practice. To do this there are a number of key ethical organisational values that should be included in a business's code of practice. These are shown below.

■ **being transparent with colleagues, customers and suppliers** – eg not hiding things in the small print of contracts, or telling customers that you can provide them with a product or service that is not available

- **reporting financial and regulatory information clearly and on time** – eg producing management accounts promptly and accurately for use by colleagues in the business

- **being open and honest by identifying when it is appropriate to accept and give gifts and hospitality** – eg defining including specific policies in the organisation's code of practice that gifts can only be accepted if they are less than £20 in value

- **paying suppliers a fair price and on time** – eg ensuring that all suppliers regardless of size are paid to terms, eg within a 30 day period of receiving an invoice

- **providing fair treatment, decent wages and good working conditions for employees** – eg ensuring that a regular review is carried out for staff who work on computer terminals to ensure their workstations comply with health and safety regulations

- **using social media** – eg ensuring that members of staff do not use social media to say offensive things about other competitors

conflict with personal values

In addition to complying with the organisation's ethical values and principles a professional accountant must ensure that he/she is able to apply his/her own ethical values and fundamental principles to decide whether behaviour is ethical or unethical.

Although many organisations have well defined codes of conduct and business ethics there may be occasions where the key personal values of an individual within the organisation may conflict with the values of the organisation itself. In these circumstances it is important that the individual makes his/her feeling known and discusses the conflict with management in the business using the conflict resolution process detailed in Chapter 3.

NON COMPLIANCE

As we have seen, in addition to complying with regulations businesses introduce codes of practice and organisational values to try and ensure that its employees work ethically. But what happens if organisations and individuals do not comply with these values, codes and regulations? We will now look at the consequences of non-compliance.

non compliance by an organisation

It is one thing to produce a set of ethical organisational values however, these are only of any use if the organisation actually follows them. It is no use simply 'paying lip service' to a code of practice. The image and reputation of a business will be adversely affected if it does not comply with its values and codes. We will now look at each of the key ethical values highlighted in the previous section to see examples of the consequences of failing to comply to each of these organisational values.

- **being transparent with colleagues, customers and suppliers** – if an organisation hides unreasonable terms in the small print of a contract that they later try and enforce this will put customers off trading with that business in the future. Similarly, if a business is not clear in its dealings with suppliers these suppliers will be reluctant to deal with the business in the future

- **reporting financial and regulatory information clearly and on time** – failure to produce accurate and timely financial information may lead to poor decisions being made by the management of the business. Failure to produce regulatory information such as financial statements on time can lead to the business being fined

- **being open and honest by identifying when it is appropriate to accept and give gifts and hospitality** – a business that gives gifts or hospitality to customers could be seen as trying to influence the customer's decisions or even to bribe the customer. Similarly, accepting gifts from a supplier could influence the decision-making of the organisation. The consequence of not having clear policies regarding gifts and hospitality could be to adversely affect the image of the business and potentially lead to accusations of unethical business dealings

- **paying suppliers a fair price and on time** – a business that tries to squeeze the lowest price out of a supplier and delays payment can adversely affect the relationship with that supplier. Recently some of the large supermarkets have received some very negative publicity in the press for their control over small farmers and demanding very low prices

- **providing fair treatment, decent wages and good working conditions for employees** – if a business does not treat its employees well they will leave the organisation which will lead to high staff turnover. Also poor working conditions will affect staff morale and affect the quality of work and the commitment of the business's staff

Organisational values and codes of practice are implemented within the organisation and are not legally enforceable, however; if a business fails to comply with regulations it could be subject to fines. For example, if an organisation is found in court to have breached the Health and Safety at Work Act and its relevant statutory provisions, the court can impose significant penalties on the business.

internal disciplinary procedures by an employer

Like any employee if a professional accountant fails to adhere to the employer's organisational values or internal codes of practice the employer may bring disciplinary procedures against him/her. These disciplinary procedures should be formally documented but will normally include some or all of the following stages.

- a verbal warning
- a written warning
- a disciplinary hearing
- the opportunity to appeal
- suspension from work
- dismissal

The extent of the disciplinary action that is taken will depend on the seriousness of the breach. For example accepting a crate of wine from a client may result in the accountant receiving a verbal warning, particularly if it is the first time that he/she has done so. If, on the other hand, the accountant has committed an illegal act such as fraud this is likely to result in dismissal.

disciplinary action by professional accounting bodies

The professional accounting bodies in the UK expect their members to comply with the code of ethics and to uphold the high standards that are expected of the accounting profession. Failure by an accountant to comply with applicable regulations and codes of practice may result in the accountant being disciplined. Disciplinary action for misconduct can be taken by the individual accounting bodies and also by the Financial Reporting Council (FRC), which is the independent disciplinary body for accountants, accountancy firms and actuaries in the UK.

Misconduct falls into two main categories:

- bringing the accounting profession into disrepute
- acting in breach of the rules and regulations of the accountant's professional body

Individual accounting bodies in the UK have published disciplinary regulations, which set out the processes and sanctions that the accounting body will carry out if a member is guilty of misconduct. The procedures will involve a disciplinary investigation followed by a decision as to whether the accountant is guilty of misconduct. Depending on the severity of the misconduct the accountant could face any of the following penalties (listed in order of severity).

- be required to give a written undertaking to refrain from continuing or repeating the misconduct in question

- be fined a sum of money not exceeding a maximum figure set by the professional accounting body

- be reprimanded or severely reprimanded

- be declared ineligible for a practicing licence

- have his/her practicing licence withdrawn

- have his/her membership suspended

- be expelled from the professional accounting body

WHISTLEBLOWING

We have looked at the consequences for a business or an individual accountant of breaching ethical codes. But what does an employee do if he/she suspects an employer, a colleague or a client has committed, or may commit, an act which is illegal or unethical? He/she must decide the appropriate reporting procedures to follow. The employee may decide to 'blow the whistle' to expose the misconduct that he/she believes has or may occur.

So what do we mean by the term '**whistleblowing**'? A whistleblower can be defined as:

> *'a person who tells someone in authority about misconduct, alleged dishonesty or illegal activity that has or may occur in an organisation.'*

The misconduct could be breaking the law for example committing a fraud, contravening regulations such as health and safety regulations or something that is contrary to public interest such as corruption. The allegations of misconduct made by a whistleblower can be made internally within the organisation or externally to regulators or to the police.

internal whistleblowing

Most whistleblowers are **internal whistleblowers**, who report misconduct on the part of a colleague to someone more senior in the organisation.

It is a big decision to internally blow the whistle on an employer or colleague. This action can have a serious impact on the individual's future employment with the business and could ultimately force him/her to resign. If he/she decides to whistleblow the following points should be considered:

- ensure that he/she knows all the facts surrounding the issue and has evidence to support the facts

- ■ follow the employer's internal procedures for reporting suspected misconduct in order to disclose the malpractice, this may involve reporting unethical behaviour and breaches of confidentiality to a prescribed internal department within the organisation

- ■ ensure that the situation is fully explained to management including the concerns that he/she has and how the organisation could be affected if they are not addressed

external whistleblowing

An individual is advised to raise concerns internally before going outside of the business. However if he/she feels that the issue is not being addressed or that the matter is so serious that it cannot be raised internally he/she should report to an appropriate regulator such as the Financial Reporting Council (FRC). Legal protection available to an external whistle-blower is limited so it is important to seek third-party advice before blowing the whistle. The AAT Ethics Advice line will be able to help in these circumstances.

This can be a very serious step especially if the employee decides not to resign after blowing the whistle. In these circumstances the employer is unlikely to be very happy if one of its employees has reported them for something illegal and are unlikely to want the person to work for them any longer. Consequently is it important that the employee has some protection from dismissal if they choose to blow the whistle on the employer.

The Public Interest Disclosure Act, 1998 (PIDA) offers the employee such protection in certain circumstances. The PIDA (which is sometimes referred to as 'the Whistleblowers Charter') gives an employee protection where he/she discloses otherwise confidential information which he/she reasonably believes shows that one of the following has or is likely to occur:

- ■ a criminal offence

- ■ a breach of a legal obligation

- ■ a miscarriage of justice

- ■ endangerment of an individual's health and safety

- ■ environmental damage

In order to be protected from dismissal the employee must also be able to show that:

- ■ the disclosure is made in good faith

- ■ the employee reasonably believes that the information disclosed is true

- ■ the employee would otherwise be victimised or the evidence concealed or destroyed if the information is not disclosed

The Public Interest Disclosure Act, 1998 does make it easier for an employee to report an unethical or disreputable employer, but it still cannot offer complete protection from the employer who is the target of the whistleblowing. Recent cases of whistleblowing have resulted in employees being suspended pending an enquiry, or being dismissed at a later date. The main risk for an individual who has blown the whistle on an employer is the subsequent effect on future career prospects.

The following example highlights the serious consequences of deciding to 'blow the whistle' on an employer.

---

example

time to blow the whistle?

Stephanie Andrews works as an accountant for Harmsworthy Plc, a large quoted company. The Finance Director has asked her to help her with a scheme which she and the Managing Director have come up with. The directors have offered to pay Stephanie £5,000 for her help in the scheme which involves illegal dealing in shares of Harmsworthy. The Finance Director has made it clear to Stephanie that if she does not help them she will lose her job.

What should Stephanie do in this situation?

An employee cannot legitimately be required to break the law by his/her employer. In the first instance, Stephanie should raise her concerns with the directors of Harmsworthy and make every effort to persuade them not to break the law. However, this option could prove difficult for Stephanie as it is the senior management of Harmsworthy who are involved in the illegal activity.

Assuming Stephanie does not agree to break the law she is faced with two options. First, she could choose to resign from Harmsworthy stating her reasons for doing so. Secondly, she may decide to blow the whistle on the management of Harmsworthy and report them to the appropriate authorities. Under the second option she must be sure that the facts are correct and that she would be victimised and the evidence concealed or destroyed if she did not whistleblow.

This example highlights just how difficult it can be to make the decision to 'blow the whistle' and disclose confidential information about an employer.

seeking advice

If an accountant has exhausted all internal routes to report unethical behaviour by an employer, colleague, client or customer he/she may need to seek advice externally.

There are several organisations that can provide confidential advice including the Citizens Advice Bureau. There is also Public Concern at Work, a charity that works to support employees in the workplace by giving guidance and support about wrongdoing or malpractice in the workplace. They will help and give advice on how to raise a concern with your employer.

Like all the professional accounting bodies the AAT has a (free) ethics helpline that is available to give advice and guidance based on the ethical code. Before whistleblowing, a member of the AAT should seek confidential advice from this helpline about how to report unethical behaviour.

MONEY LAUNDERING

a definition of money laundering

In Chapter 5 we looked at the disclosure of confidential information where there has been an infringement of the law. The example we used for this was money laundering which was defined as:

'to move illegally acquired cash through financial systems so that it appears to be legally acquired'.

Put simply, this means using money gained illegally – eg through terrorist funding, drug dealing or other criminal activities – so that the money is 'laundered' or 'washed' and then appears to be 'clean' and legally obtained.

Activities related to money laundering include:

- acquiring, using or possessing criminal property
- handling the proceeds of crime such as theft, fraud and tax evasion
- being knowingly involved in any way with criminal or terrorist property
- entering into arrangements to facilitate laundering criminal or terrorist property
- investing the proceeds of crime into other financial products
- investing the proceeds of crime into the acquisition of property/assets
- transferring criminal property

Criminal property is property which was knowingly obtained as a result of criminal conduct. It may take a number of forms including money, security, tangible or intangible property. Terrorist property is money or property likely to be used for terrorist purposes, or the process of commissioning or carrying out terrorist acts.

An accountant will be guilty of a money laundering offence if he/she provides accounting services while 'turning a blind eye' to the client's suspect dealings. This would be viewed as facilitating the client's illegal activities as detailed in the fourth point above. The value of the criminal property will have no bearing on whether or not an accountant should report a money laundering offence as there is no de minimis exceptions or lower limit in relation to money laundering or terrorist financing offences.

Similarly, a professional accountant in business must be vigilant in preventing and detecting money laundering in the organisation he/she works for.

The example below illustrates a situation where an accountant has to consider money laundering.

> **example**
>
> Your client Eric has been given some company shares by his aunt, who bought them with money that she did not declare to the tax authorities (ie tax evasion). By accepting these shares is Eric guilty of money laundering? Are you as his accountant guilty of a money laundering offence?
>
> The shares will only be criminal property as far as Eric is concerned if he knows or suspects that they had originally been acquired as a result of criminal conduct on the part of his aunt. He will then commit a money laundering offence if he deals in them. Conversely, if he has no knowledge or suspicion regarding the funds that his aunt used to purchase the shares then he will not be committing an offence.
>
> As his accountant you are in a similar position in that you will only be committing a money laundering offence if you know or suspect that the shares are criminal property. As Eric's accountant you can still be found guilty of money laundering if you knew about the criminal property even if Eric is innocent as your client's state of mind has no bearing on your obligations.

money laundering rules

The legislation and regulations relating to money laundering, or anti-money laundering legislation can be found in the following laws and regulations:

The Proceeds of Crime Act 2002 (POCA): this sets out the principal money laundering offence and the requirements to report suspicious transactions.

The Terrorism Act 2000 (TA): this sets out the principal terrorist financing offences and reporting obligations in similar terms to POCA.

The Money Laundering Regulations 2007 (the Regulations): these require sole traders and firms to establish procedures intended to detect and prevent activities relating to money laundering and terrorist financing.

national crime agency

As the name suggests the National Crime Agency (NCA) is a crime-fighting law enforcement agency responsible for pro-active operations against serious and organised crime. NCA tackles serious organised crime that affects the UK and its citizens including class A drugs, people smuggling, human trafficking, major gun crime, fraud, computer crime and money laundering.

money laundering penalties

Under the laws and regulations above an individual found guilty of money laundering, or the organisation that he/she works for, can be penalised.

Dependent on the severity of the offence this could be an unlimited fine and/or a prison sentence of up to fourteen years.

the accountant's duty to report money laundering

The **Proceeds of Crime Act 2002 (POCA)** and the **Terrorism Act 2000**, require accountants as individuals in the regulated sector to report any suspicion that a client, employer or colleague is involved with criminal property to the National Crime Agency (NCA) in a suspicious activity report (SAR). If the accountant is working in an organisation which, due to its size, has appointed a Money Laundering Reporting Officer (MLRO), the matter should be reported to the MLRO in an internal report. The MLRO will then review the information they have received and decide if it needs to be reported to the NCA.

Once the nominated officer decides there are reasonable grounds to suspect money laundering they must tell the NCA at the earliest possible opportunity. The nominated officer should get consent from the NCA to complete the transaction. If it's not possible to delay the transaction to get consent, the nominated officer should inform the NCA of this when they send their report.

terrorist financing

Terrorist financing is the provision or collection of funds from legitimate or illegitimate sources with the intention or in the knowledge that they should be used in order to carry out any act of terrorism, whether or not those funds are in fact used for that purpose. Like money laundering the maximum penalty for this offence is an unlimited fine and /or up to 14 years in prison.

The following example highlights a situation where an accountant may suspect money laundering.

example

terrorist financing

Julia is a qualified accountant who works as a sole practitioner. She has recently started work on the year-end accounts for her client Michael. During her work she discovers a number of payments that have been made to an overseas company that she does not recognise. There is no detailed supporting documentation for these payments. Julia suspects that these payments may relate to terrorists activities.

What should Julia do in these circumstances?

As Julia is a sole practitioner she will not have a Money Laundering Reporting Office (MLRO) to whom she can report her concerns. She should, therefore, report her concerns to NCA using a Suspicious Activity Report (SAR). Failure to do this could result in Julia being charged with terrorist financing offences. She should not inform Michael of her suspicions.

required disclosure

There are two circumstances where a **required disclosure** in an internal report or a SAR **must** be made by an accountant:

■ when the accountant wishes to provide services to a client in relation to property which is known or suspected to relate to money laundering or terrorist financing. In such circumstances, the person making the report must indicate in the report that he/she is asking for consent to provide such services. He/she cannot provide the services until consent is received

■ when the accountant actually knows or suspects, or there are reasonable objective grounds for knowing or suspecting that another person is engaged in money laundering or terrorist financing, regardless of whether or not he/she wishes to act for that person. The person in question could be a client, colleague or a third party

As a minimum the standard report or SAR must contain:

■ the identity of the suspected person (if known), such as, full name, address, telephone numbers, passport details, date of birth, account details

■ the information on which the suspicion of money laundering is based

■ the whereabouts of the laundered property if it is known

■ details of the person making the report which will normally be the MLRO or sole practitioner

One particular area where this must be considered is where, despite advice from his/her accountant, the client has failed to disclose an omission or error in his/her tax affairs. Although it would seem logical to report this to HMRC, an accountant should report this to the firm's MLRO or if he/she is a sole practitioner, to NCA.

If an accountant believes that a fraud had been committed then he/she also has a duty to report this to the police.

Practices and employers must also have training and internal procedures in place to ensure that they comply with the reporting requirements above. If these procedures are not in place the accountant may be liable for a fine or imprisonment or both.

Clearly this is an important legal issue that the accounting profession takes very seriously. Professional accountants and students must ensure that they are familiar with their employer's internal procedures for reporting suspicions of money laundering. Employers must ensure that all their staff have been provided with adequate training on their legal obligations in respect of money laundering and the firms anti-money laundering procedures.

protected and authorised disclosure

Where any person, not just an accountant, submits a report providing a required disclosure of a suspicion of money laundering this is a **protected disclosure**. This means that the person is protected against allegations of breach of confidentiality regardless of how the restriction on the disclosure of the confidential information was originally imposed. For example, as we saw in Chapter 5, an accountant has an ongoing duty of confidentiality to his/her client. If, however, the accountant has had to include confidential information about the client in a SAR that he/she submits, the accountant is protected against any allegations of breaches of confidentiality that the client might make.

Any person, not just an accountant, who realises that they may have engaged or are about to engage in money laundering, should make an **authorised disclosure** to the appropriate authority. The disclosure should be made before the act is carried out (and he/she has obtained consent for the act from NCA, see required disclosure above), or as soon after the act is done with good reason for the delay. This may then provide him/her with a defence against charges of money laundering.

exceptions to the duty to report

There are certain circumstances where an accountant is **not** obliged to report knowledge or suspicions of money laundering. These are:

- when the information that forms the basis of the knowledge or suspicion was obtained other than in the course of the accountant's business, for example during a social occasion
- when the information came about in privileged circumstances, that resulted from the accountant being asked to provide legal advice, expert opinion or services in relation to legal proceedings. An example of this would be if an accountant found out information about possible money laundering whilst explaining the client's tax liability. However, a report would have to be made if the advice sought from the accountant was to enable the client to commit a criminal offence or to avoid detection
- when there is a reasonable excuse for not reporting straightaway. In this case the report must be made as soon as reasonable in the circumstances. There is currently no money laundering case law relating to 'reasonable excuse' and it is anticipated that would only be accepted in relatively extreme circumstances, such as duress and threats to safety

failure to disclose

We have already discussed the requirement for an accountant to report his/her suspicion of money laundering to the firm's MLRO or directly to

NCA. However, it is worth noting that it is an offence of **'failure to disclose'** under the POCA if an accountant does not report his/her suspicion. This offence carries a maximum penalty of five years imprisonment and/or a fine.

prejudicing an investigation

A further money laundering offence may be committed where any person, not just an accountant, knows or suspects that a money laundering investigation is being conducted or is about to be conducted and either:

- makes a disclosure which is likely to **prejudice the investigation**; or
- falsifies, conceals or destroys documents relating to the investigation, or causes this to happen.

The person making the disclosure does not have to intend to prejudice an investigation for the offence to apply. However, it is worth noting that there is a defence available if the person making the disclosure did not know or suspect the disclosure would be prejudicial, did not know or suspect that the documents were relevant, or did not intend to conceal facts from the person carrying out the investigation.

tipping off

POCA has created a criminal offence of **'tipping off'**. This is where an accountant who knows, or thinks they know that, a report of money laundering has been made to a MLRO, NCA, HMRC or the police, warns (or 'tips off') the person(s) suspected. Where this happens the person who 'tips off' the suspect is liable to be prosecuted as well as the person who is carrying out the money laundering. The person who tips off does not have to intend to prejudice an investigation for this offence to apply.

An accountant who discovers that an employer or a client is potentially money laundering must report his/her suspicions to the Money Laundering Reporting Officer or NCA. They must ensure, however, that they do not make the employer or client aware of this as this would be considered tipping off.

Although tipping off is an offence, an accountant is entitled to advise his/her clients in general terms about the issue of money laundering.

The maximum penalty for tipping off is 5 years imprisonment and/or a fine.

The following example illustrates the serious implications of money laundering.

example

a case of money laundering

Wilfred Joyce is an accountant in public practice. One of his clients is an antiques dealer called Louis Kans. One Friday Wilfred receives a telephone enquiry from Louis, who says that a customer is in the shop asking to buy a piece of furniture for £11,000. The customer is offering to pay Louis in cash.

What should Wilfred advise in this situation?

Louis has been offered a large amount of cash but does not really know where it has come from. Although the customer may have good reasons for having such a large amount of cash there is a risk that it may not have been gained through legal means.

As Wilfred's objective in this situation is to ensure that his client does not breach the Money Laundering Regulations 2007, he should advise Louis to identify the customer and verify the source of the cash before accepting it, thus satisfying himself that the cash is not the proceeds of some crime.

If despite Wilfred's advice Louis then goes on and deals with the customer on a cash basis then Wilfred will have no option but to report him to NCA.

customer due diligence

Before providing services to a client, accountants must consider whether their services could be used to facilitate money laundering or to finance terrorist activities. The Money Laundering Regulations 2007 identifies several situations where an accountant must carry out **customer due diligence** (CDD). These situations include: before the accountant enters into a business relationship with a new client; when the accountant suspects that money laundering or terrorist financing might be taking place; where the accountant is dubious about information that the client has previously given him/her about the client's identity or when the accountant is entering into a transaction with the client for a significant amount of money.

One definition of due diligence is:

'the process of evaluating a prospective business decision by investigating relevant financial, legal, and other important information about the other party.'

Therefore, in order to carry out sufficient CDD the accountant must have a detailed look at the client and the way it operates to decide whether he/she can enter into a professional relationship with the client, confident that there are no ethical issues or any risk that they may be involved in money laundering.

CDD should include:

- verifying the client's identity by looking at documents, data or other information obtained from a reliable source
- where the person who owns the business is not the person who runs it, the accountant should ensure that he/she fully understands who any beneficial owners are (normally defined as someone who owns 25% or more of the business). In this case the accountant should also carry out the same sort of verification of the identity of the owner
- the accountant should also find out what the client wants from the relationship or the purpose and nature of the transaction

Where the accountant is unable to carry out adequate CDD he/she must decline the assignment. If, having carried out due diligence, the accountant has a suspicion that the client may be involved in money laundering or terrorist financing, the accountant must submit a report to the Money Laundering Reporting Officer or submit a Suspicious Activity Report to the National Crime Agency (NCA).

The following example illustrates how due diligence would be carried out in practice.

example

Gill Gardener is a partner in Gardner & Shah, a firm of accountants. She has been approached by Mike McGann, the manager and co-owner of a small chain of local fish and chips shops, to act as his accountant. What does Gill have to do before she can enter into a professional relationship with Mike?

Gill must verify Mike's identity. The best way to do this is to ask Mike if she can see his passport, making sure that she fully explains to him why she needs to do this. She should also verify the identity of Mike's co-owner in the same way.

Finally, she should discuss with Mike exactly what he wants from the professional relationship with Gardner and Shah. In practice these discussions will probably take place during the negotiations between Gill and Mike and details will be included in the letter of engagement.

Provided Gill carries out sufficient due diligence and she is happy with the identity of Mike and his partner she can enter into a professional relationship with Mike.

keeping records of customer due diligence

The Money Laundering Regulations are very clear about the circumstances where it is necessary for customer due diligence (CDD) to be carried out. The regulations also require that records of CDD that has been performed should be maintained to assist in any future law enforcement investigating relating to clients. These records will also demonstrate that the accountant has complied with his/her statutory obligations. Records of CDD carried out should include:

- copies of or reference to the CDD evidence that was used to verify the client's identity, for example passport details. These records must be kept for five years starting with the date on which the accountant's relationship with the client ends

- copies or originals of documents relating to transactions that have been subject to CDD or to ongoing monitoring, for example an invoice supporting a client receipt of a large cash payment from a customer. These must be kept for five years starting from the date on which the accountant completed the client's instructions

INAPPROPRIATE CLIENT BEHAVIOUR

We have looked in detail at the offences of money laundering and terrorist financing and the need for an accountant to be vigilant in identifying and reporting potential or actual instances of this. These offences could be on the part of an employee, colleague or client. We are now going to summarise the specific issues facing an accountant in practice when he/she identifies inappropriate client behaviour.

reporting inappropriate client behaviour

An accountant in practice will report actual or suspected money laundering to the Money Laundering Reporting Officer (MLRO), if the business has one, or directly to NCA. An accountant may also identify other inappropriate client behaviour, including fraud or other illegal acts. In these circumstances the accountant must ensure that this is reported to the appropriate person or the relevant authority. In the case of fraud or other illegal acts the matter must be raised with the police.

If the accountant is not sure how to proceed, he/she should raise the issue with a more senior member of staff in the firm. Larger accounting practices will have dedicated helplines that their staff can contact if they need further advice on dealing with inappropriate client behaviour that the accountant feels could be illegal or unethical. If the accountant works for a small firm or is a sole practitioner, advice is available from his/her professional accounting body's helpline. An example of this is the AAT Ethics Advice line.

Failure to act appropriately in response to inappropriate client behaviour can result in the accountant being accused of offences such as of 'tipping off' or 'failure to disclose'.

threats and safeguards

In Chapter 2 we looked at the types of threats that an accountant faces to his/her fundamental ethical principles. These were categorised as follows:

- self-interest threats
- self-review threats
- familiarity threats
- intimidation threats
- advocacy threats

When dealing with clients, an accountant in practice must be particularly mindful of familiarity, intimidation and advocacy threats and ensure that safeguards are in place to mitigate these threats.

Familiarity threats may occur where the relationship between the accountant and the client is too close or 'familiar'. This could be because of an actual relationship or friendship or as a result of the accountant working for the client for a number of years and becoming friendlier and more sympathetic to the interests of the client. A professional accountant must ensure that he/she safeguards his/her objectivity.

Intimidation threats may occur if the client or a member of the client's management is a dominant personality. The client may threaten to dismiss the accountant or not award work to the accountant if he/she does not do what the client demands. If the accountant works for a larger firm of accountants this should be reported to more senior management in the firm. They can then decide what action to take, including the possibility of replacing the accountant with a stronger personality to counter the intimidation threats. A sole practitioner will have to be firm with the client, however, if the threats cannot be eliminated or reduced to an acceptable level then the sole practitioner may have to resign from the assignment.

Advocacy threats result from an accountant supporting the position or opinion of a client to the point that his/her objectivity may be compromised. Accountants must be careful not to be pressurised into supporting or promoting a client's position and refuse if they feel their fundamental principles are being threatened.

Examples of safeguards against these types of threats were detailed in Chapter 2.

Chapter Summary

- Many businesses have their own codes of conduct and codes of practice which help individuals in the organisation to make the right choice when faced with an ethical dilemma.

- Individuals who work in an organisation will be influenced by the management's attitude to ethics; the tone at the top will have a trickledown effect on the people who work in it.

- Organisations should comply with 'the spirit' of regulations and should include key ethical organisational values in its code of practice. These are:
  - Being transparent with colleagues, customers and suppliers
  - Reporting financial and regulatory information clearly and on time
  - Being open and honest by identifying when it is appropriate to accept and give gifts and hospitality
  - Paying suppliers a fair price and on time
  - Providing fair treatment, decent wages and good working conditions for employees

- Failure to comply with an employer's organisational values or codes of practice can result in an accountant being disciplined by his/her employer or professional accounting body.

- Accountants and other employees may decide to report illegal or unethical behaviour on the part of an employer, colleague or client through the process of whistleblowing.

- Providing a member is acting in good faith when they 'blow the whistle' on an employer and so break the duty of confidentiality, he/she will be protected in many situations by the Public Interest Disclosure Act 1998.

- If an accountant has knowledge or a suspicion that a client or an employer is money laundering they must report this to the National Crime Agency (NCA), or to the firm's Money Laundering Reporting Officer.

- The money laundering rules are set out in the Proceeds of Crime Act 2002, The Terrorism Act 2000 and the Money Laundering Regulations 2007.

- The maximum penalty if convicted of money laundering is 14 years imprisonment.

- A required disclosure of a suspicion of money laundering is a protected disclosure, which means the person is protected against allegations of breach of confidentiality.

- There are certain exceptions to the duty to report knowledge or suspicion of money laundering.

- Failure to disclose a suspicion of money laundering carries a maximum penalty of 5 years imprisonment or a fine.

■   It is an offence for an individual to make a disclosure which is likely to prejudice an investigation into money laundering or to falsify, conceal or destroy documents relating to the investigation.

■   It is a criminal offence to tell someone that they may be investigated for possible money laundering. This is the offence of 'tipping off' and carries a maximum penalty of 5 years imprisonment and/or a fine.

■   Accountants should carry out customer due diligence before providing services to a client to ensure there are no legal or ethical reasons why they should not enter into a professional relationship with the client. In particular the accountant should ensure that his/her services are not being used to facilitate money laundering.

■   Where an accountant identifies instances of inappropriate client behaviour he/she should raise the issue with a more senior member of staff in the firm or contact his/her professional accounting body's helpline.

Key Terms

business ethics and codes of conduct	guidelines drawn up by an individual organisation which set out its values and governs decisions and actions in that organisation
tone at the top	the ethical atmosphere that is created in the workplace by the organisation's leadership
disciplinary action	processes and sanctions that a professional accounting body can carry out if a member is accused of non-compliance with its regulations and the code of ethics
internal whistleblowing	telling someone more senior within the organisation about something illegal or unethical within the organisation that the employee works for
Public Interest Disclosure Act 1998 (PIDA)	a statute that protects employees who make disclosures of confidential information that they believe to be in the public interest
money laundering	moving illegally acquired cash through financial systems so that it appear to be legally acquired
Proceeds of Crime Act 2002	a statute that sets out the law in relation to financial gains made from illegal acts

Terrorism Act (2000)	a statute that sets out the law in relation to terrorism financing
Money Laundering Regulations 2007	the regulations governing the crime of money laundering
National Crime Agency	NCA is a crime-fighting law enforcement agency responsible for proactive operations against serious and organised crime including money laundering
Suspicious Activity Report	a report submitted to NCA giving details of suspected money laundering
required disclosure	disclosure of money laundering must be made when an accountant knows or suspects money laundering on the part of a client
protected disclosure	disclosure of a suspicion of money laundering is protected against allegations of breach of confidentiality
authorised disclosure	disclosure by a person who realises they may have engaged in money laundering or are about to engage in money laundering
failure to disclose	failure to tell the relevant authority about a suspicion or knowledge of money laundering
prejudicing an investigation	making a disclosure that is likely to adversely affect an investigation into suspected money laundering
tipping off	the criminal offence of warning an individual that he/she is suspected of money laundering
customer due diligence	evaluating prospective business decisions by investigating relevant financial, legal and other important information about the other party

Activities

6.1 Clearview Ltd has recently decided to produce a code of practice to use within its finance and payroll function. This is in response to guidelines produced by its trade organisation.

Once it has been implemented explain whether this will be a statutory code of practice.

6.2 List the **five** key organisational ethical values that a business should include in its code of practice.

1	
2	
3	
4	
5	

6.3 Martin is a member of the AAT who works for Mejanna Ltd. His manager has recently overheard Martin in the pub telling a friend all about a confidential matter at work. The manager has told Martin that he will now face disciplinary procedures because he has behaved unethically.

Decide whether or not each of the following organisations can bring disciplinary procedures against Martin for his unethical behaviour.

	Can	**Cannot**
(a) The National Crime Agency (NCA)		
(b) Mejanna Ltd		
(c) AAT		

Select **one** option for each organisation.

6.4 Felicity believes that her colleague, Marcus, has acted illegally and has decided to internally whistleblow on Marcus's misconduct.

What points should Felicity consider before she decides whether to whistleblow?

6.5   **(a)**   State the **three** key pieces of legislation and regulations that relate to money laundering.

1	
2	
3	

(b)   State the maximum penalties that an individual could face if found guilty of money laundering.

(c)   What name is given to the person in an organisation to whom a suspicion of money laundering should be reported?

6.6   Ashleigh is a qualified accountant who works for Riley & Khan an accounting practice in Powerbridge. Below are three situations which have occurred at Riley & Khan this week.

For each one explain whether Ashleigh should carry out customer due diligence (CDD) procedures.

(a)   One of Riley & Khan's clients, Voltec Ltd has informed Ashleigh that they need her help to apply for a permanent license to sell alcohol online. Voltec are a business that manufactures and fits double glazed windows and doors.

(b)   Riley and Khan have been the accountants for Oscar's a local restaurant in Powerbridge for a number of years. Oscar Price, the proprietor, has recently taken on a new partner in the business, Simeon Gray, who now holds a 55% share of Oscar's. Oscar will continue running the restaurant on a day-to-day basis.

(c)   Dennis James is a client of Riley & Khan. Ashleigh has completed Dennis's personal tax return for each of the last four years, and always holds the money in a client account for Dennis before paying HMRC on the due date. Dennis has now asked Ashleigh to complete his wife Helena's tax return and hold the money for her to pay HMRC. Ashleigh has met Helena socially on a number of occasions.

6.7   Georgia is a qualified accountant who works as a sole practitioner. She has just started work on a new client, Opino Ltd. When she took on Opino Ltd as a client she carried out appropriate customer due diligence procedures. Georgia is now completing the VAT Return for Opino Ltd for the current quarter and has found a significant error in the previous quarter's return which has resulted in a large underpayment of VAT by Opino. This return was completed by their previous accountant, Joe.

Georgia raises this issue with Edgar, the owner of Opino who replies 'Well if HMRC haven't noticed we won't need to adjust it! I'll tell Joe to keep quiet about it'. Despite Georgia strongly advising him to disclose the error to HMRC, he refuses.

(a)   Explain what Georgia must do in this situation.

(b)   What are the consequences for Georgia if she does not take any action in this situation?

(c)   What action should Joe take regarding Edgar's refusal to disclose the error to HMRC?

6.8   Jake works for Delaney & Clarke, a firm of accountants in Sandsville. He has recently been working on the accounts for one of his clients Thompson Facilities Ltd that provides security services at large outdoor events. Jake has noticed some unusual large cash transactions going through its accounts for which he cannot find any supporting paperwork. He strongly suspects that the money has come from sales on which Thompson Facilities Ltd has not charged VAT.

What are the consequences for Jake if he raises the issue of the unusual cash transactions with the management of Thompson Facilities Ltd?

7 Sustainability

this chapter covers...

This chapter will look at the need for organisations to operate in a sustainable manner and to protect sustainable development. The chapter goes on to explain the Brundtland report's definition of sustainable development. It then explains what is meant by 'the triple bottom line' ie the three components of sustainable development which are:

■ economic growth

■ environmental protection

■ social equality

The last part of the chapter will focus on the responsibility of professional accountants to uphold the principles of sustainability throughout all aspects of their work.

AN INTRODUCTION TO SUSTAINABILITY

what is sustainability?

One definition of sustainability is '**the ability to last**'. Over recent years the UK government has placed increased emphasis on the importance of 'green' policies for organisations and individuals. This ranges from encouraging recycling by households and businesses, to the government's own commitment to reduce the country's carbon emissions. These green policies protect the environment, save energy and ultimately benefit society as a whole.

However, it is not simply 'being green' that supports sustainability and sustainable development. Organisations must ensure the responsible long-term management of the resources that they use. In addition to the environmental impact of management decisions sustainability also involves economic and social issues.

the Brundtland report

In 1983 the United Nations (UN) set up the World Commission on Environment and Development (WCED), chaired by Gro Harlem Brundtland, a former Norwegian Prime Minister. This organisation aimed to bring together the international community to pursue a common goal to support sustainability by identifying sustainability problems worldwide, raising awareness of them and suggesting and implementing solutions. The problem was that for too many years, businesses worldwide had been able to operate without restriction; their only goal being to generate profit. One of the consequences of this need for 'profit at all costs' approach was increased environmental damage.

In 1987 the **Brundtland commission**, as WCED became known, published its report 'Our Common Future.' This report defined sustainable development as:

> '*development that meets the needs of the present without compromising the ability of future generations to meet their own needs.*'

The report then went on to highlight three key components of sustainable development:

- economic growth
- environmental protection
- social equality

In the next section we will look at each of these three objectives of sustainable development in more detail.

the triple bottom line

The three elements of sustainable development that were identified by the Brundtland committee are sometimes also referred to as the **triple bottom line**. Economic growth, environmental protection and social equality may also be abbreviated to 'profit, planet and people' – an easy way to remember these three key objectives. These are explained in more detail below.

economic growth and sustainability

In order for sustainable development to happen the resources to allow it must be available. **Economic growth** provides these resources. It relates to:

■ individual countries; the growth in the economy of a country should lead to an overall increase in the wealth of that country which then benefits its population as a whole

■ individual organisations; profit generated by organisations will increase the wealth of the owners and employees

One key principle to remember is that sustainable growth relies on three factors, not simply the generation of profit. Hence economic growth should not be pursued at the expense of the two other factors. In recent years the spotlight has been on sustainability; consequently organisations are beginning to realise that cost-cutting can no longer be the number one business priority and transferring production and services to low-cost countries such as Bangladesh, China and Mexico brings with it hidden social and environmental costs. These include cheap labour and poor working conditions and excessive use of hydrocarbons (for example coal power) which adversely affects the ozone layer.

environmental protection and sustainability

The green policies of an organisation are those most commonly associated with sustainability. The **protection of the environment** is key to conserving the world's resources with organisations keen to highlight their 'green' credentials. You may have heard the phrase 'reduce, re-use, recycle'. Some examples of environmentally friendly policies that contribute to sustainability are:

■ supermarkets that reward customers for re-using plastic shopping bags, thereby reducing the number of plastic bags that end up in landfill

■ recycling paper, metal and certain plastics and also using recycled office supplies such as printer paper and printer ink cartridges

■ promoting car sharing schemes, cycle to work incentives and the use of low-emission company vehicles all reduce the 'carbon footprint' of a business and its employees

- only trading with suppliers that have certified green policies eg companies that make toilet tissue will ensure its paper suppliers replace the trees they use with new trees
- encouraging staff to reduce energy usage by turning off lights, only filling and boiling kettles with the required amount of water

Although the primary objective of an organisation's 'green' policies is to protect the environment by reducing waste and using fewer resources the organisation itself may also benefit. Using less energy and other consumables will actually save the organisation money as it will spend less on expensive resources.

social equality and sustainability

This objective of sustainability focuses on the social well-being of people. Social equality extends beyond ensuring that employees are happy and well treated in the workplace. An organisation should consider the social equality of the local community and also society as a whole. We do not have to look far to see evidence of worldwide social inequality. International news reports regularly highlight the extreme poverty and poor living conditions in certain parts of the world.

Organisations can promote social responsibility both locally and in a worldwide context in a number of ways. Some examples are listed below:

- making charitable donations which help and support the socially underprivileged
- only trading with overseas suppliers that can provide evidence of reasonable pay and decent working conditions for its staff
- supporting local initiatives to get out of work people back into work
- sponsoring local sports events that 'give something back' to the local community

CORPORATE SOCIAL RESPONSIBILITY

Increasingly, large organisations are publishing **Corporate Social Responsibility (CSR)** reports. These reports detail how the organisation takes responsibility for supporting sustainable development through it policies and procedures. It also identifies to what extent it has achieved its CSR objectives.

There is mounting pressure on businesses to be transparent in the way in which they operate and a growing number of organisations are choosing to voluntarily report on their CSR. While there is no legal requirement to produce a CSR report, businesses are realising that the public and investors are keen to see their attitude to sustainability. If an organisation can show progress towards achieving its CSR goals the public will look more favourably on the business which will enhance its reputation as an ethical organisation.

CSR initiatives that a business may adopt include:

- reducing CO_2 emission from its premises
- trading with organisations with a proven track record of good staff working conditions
- supporting charitable fundraising activities (eg matching amounts of fundraising that staff members have raised)
- making regular donations to charity
- setting recycling targets for the organisation
- promoting car-sharing schemes and 'cycle to work' initiatives
- using local suppliers where possible

An example of an organisation that produces a CSR policy that is relevant to the readers of this book is the AAT. The full AAT CSR policy can be downloaded at www.aat.org.uk/about-aat/aat-sustainability, however the key principles included in this document are shown below:

AAT recognises that its operations inevitably have an impact on wider environmental, economic and social issues. These issues are an integral part of our quality management process and we believe that placing emphasis on them gives the right message to our employees, members, suppliers and other key stakeholders and demonstrates our awareness of, and concern for, the wider community.

We are committed to continuous improvements in environmental, economic and social sustainability.

We will comply with all European law applicable to environmental legislation, regulations, approved codes of practice and other external requirements applicable to our business.

We will continuously develop our CSR policy by:

- measuring and reporting our performance
- identifying opportunities and taking action where practical to meet legal obligations and improve sustainability
- identifying adverse impacts and risks, and where possible mitigate these
- promoting our CSR policy and gain buy in from all our employees and other key stakeholders
- embedding our CSR policy and practice into all our management systems, standards, processes and procedures.

When a business is reporting on sustainability it should strike the right balance of positive and negative information. Positive information will include measurement of how the organisation has met its sustainability goals. Negative reporting will show where it has failed to reach its CSR targets or has only partially achieved its goals. Although there is a risk that reporting negative results could damage the organisation's reputation, companies are expected to report on their sustainability practices 'warts and all'. If CSR reporting is too positive there is a risk that management will be perceived as overplaying their 'green credentials'. A business that uses CSR reporting simply as a public relations exercise won't fool anyone!

THE RESPONSIBILITY OF ACCOUNTANTS TO UPHOLD SUSTAINABILITY

We have seen the importance of sustainability and sustainable development for the way in which organisations operate. We will now look at the responsibilities of finance professionals in upholding the principles of sustainability.

public interest duty

Professional accountants have public interest duties to protect society as a whole. Consequently they must consider the economic, social and environmental aspects of their work in order to support sustainability and sustainable development. This should include:

- ensuring the long-term responsible management of resources used by their organisation
- contributing to the running of their organisation in a sustainable manner
- assessing and minimising the risks to the organisation, and to society as a whole, of not acting sustainably

An accountant will be involved in the production of a significant amount of information that will be used by a wide range of stakeholders including shareholders, banks, customers, suppliers and employees. The accountant's ethical duty of integrity means that when preparing this information he/she must be transparent, ie not hide anything, and must ensure that this information is not misleading to its potential users.

Professional accountants within a business are also often involved in the introduction of Corporate Social Responsibility (CSR) policies and in reporting the success (or failure) of the business in complying with these objectives. As responsible, professionally qualified individuals they should have the skills and knowledge to report accurately on the way in which the organisation has achieved it sustainability aims and objectives.

promoting an ethics-based culture

The need to operate sustainably and to promote sustainable development goes hand-in-hand with the need to operate ethically. Sustainability inherently relies on the management of an organisation acting in an ethical manner. Professional accountants must act ethically in all aspects of their working life and in addition to this, should actively encourage and promote an ethics-based culture that discourages unethical or illegal practices, including money laundering, terrorist financing, fraud, theft, bribery, non-compliance with applicable regulations, bullying and decision-making that does not consider the longer term. In the long term these factors may have an impact on a business's continued operation as well as potentially having an impact on society and the environment. This should be both within the organisation that the accountant works for and for accountants in practice, when they are dealing with clients.

promoting sustainability

Accountants should promote (champion) the aim for organisations to ensure sustainable development within the organisation that he/she works for. For an accountant in practice he/she should encourage clients to support sustainable development. However, accountants must also remain objective, a fundamental ethical principle that we looked at in detail in Chapter 3. This means that they should give equal consideration to all relevant issues before making a decision. This need for objectivity is still important when an accountant is promoting sustainability in the organisation. The accountant should not necessarily support sustainability initiatives simply because something fulfils CSR objectives: he/she should consider what other effects the introduction of this initiative will have on the effective operation of the business.

reputational risk

As we have seen earlier in this chapter the attitude of a business to sustainability can have a significant impact on its reputation with its wider stakeholders. This can be investors, employees, customers and suppliers. Failure to act sustainably can have an adverse effect on the reputation of the business. However, sustainable development will have a positive effect on the organisation's reputation as ethical and sustainably aware.

consider the triple bottom line

The Brundtland report identifies the three key objectives for sustainability, often referred to as the 'triple bottom line'. These are:

■ economic growth

■ environmental protection

■ social equality

Accountants are frequently involved in providing information for management decision-making. Historically this information has focused on the success of the business measured primarily on profitability and growth of the organisation. However, in recent years there has been a shift in reporting so that not only financial measures are used to assess success. The sustainability initiatives that the business has introduced and the extent to which it has managed to achieve them is also considered a measure of success. Consequently professional accountants must ensure that the triple bottom line is considered as part of their reporting on the performance of the business and that sustainable development is activity encouraged.

This means that in addition to promoting economic/financial aspects when measuring an organisation's income, expenses, assets and liabilities, accountants should also promote social and environmental aspects. For example an accountant may be asked to provide information about how to reduce costs by buying raw materials from overseas. When the accountant does this he/she should also report on whether the production of these raw materials overseas is done responsibly, with good pay and working conditions to the employees that produce it.

promoting sustainable practices

Accountants must also promote sustainable practices through the organisation in relation to each of the following:

- products and services – eg ensuring that the products or services supplied by the organisations are produced from sustainably resourced materials and that suppliers' staff have fair pay and decent working conditions

- customers – eg businesses should supply to their customers in a sustainable manner, through efficient delivery methods, and fair long-term pricing strategies

- employees – eg encouraging staff to take appropriate qualifications and providing them with good working conditions

- the workplace – eg implementing green policies relating to recycling and conservation of energy and then monitoring the participation of staff in the schemes as a measure of their success

- the supply chain – eg encouraging their organisation or clients to source supplies from suppliers with an ethical approach to sustainability

- business functions and processes –accountants should constantly review the way in which the business operates to ensure that it continues to be operating in a responsible way that supports and encourages sustainability and sustainable development

raising awareness of social responsibility

The professional accounting bodies in the UK include sustainability as part of the assessments and examination for students wishing to qualify with them; this Unit is an example of this. Qualified professional accountants are expected to promote the need for corporate social responsibility (CSR) and to encourage employers and clients to assess the impact of their decisions and actions on sustainable development in the future. For example, this may be through ethical buying decisions or encouraging recycling initiatives.

Chapter Summary

■ The need for sustainability and sustainable development was highlighted by the Brundtland report which was published in 1987 and defined sustainable development as:

'development that meets the needs of the present without compromising the ability of future generations to meet their own needs.'

■ The three objectives of sustainable development are:

– economic growth

– environmental protection

– social equality

■ These three objectives are often known as the 'triple bottom line'.

■ Some organisations now publish Corporate Social Responsibility (CSR) reports that show the extent to which they have met their sustainability targets and objectives.

■ Professional accountants have a responsibility to uphold sustainability in the workplace.

■ Accountants' public interest duties to protect society as a whole means that they must consider the economic, social and environmental aspect of their work to support sustainability.

■ Accountants should promote an ethics-based culture.

■ It is important for professional accountants to remain objective when championing sustainability.

■ An organisation's attitude to sustainability will have a direct effect on the reputation of the organisation.

■ Accountants must take into account the triple bottom line of social, environmental and ethical factors when measuring the performance of an organisation and when assisting decision-making.

■ Professional accountants should promote sustainable practices and raise awareness of social responsibility in their workplace.

Key Terms	**sustainable development**	development that meets the needs of the present without compromising the ability of future generations to meet their own needs
	Brundtland report	a report entitled 'Our Common Future' issued by a commission of the United Nations which aimed to pursue a common goal to support sustainability worldwide
	triple bottom line	the three components of sustainable development: economic growth, environmental protection and social equality
	corporate social responsibility (CSR)	objectives and policies adopted by an organisation to support sustainability and sustainable development
	public interest	the welfare of the general public in which the whole of society has a stake
	reputational risk	a risk of loss resulting from damage to an organisation's reputation which could be as a result of a poor attitude to sustainable development

Activities

7.1 The UN Brundtland report on sustainability and sustainable development identifies three key objectives of sustainability and sustainable development.

(a) State these three objectives and give one example of how a business can support each one.

1 Objective: Example
2 Objective: Example
3 Objective: Example

(b) State the definition of sustainable development as set out in the Brundtland report.

7.2 Organisations publish reports detailing their success in supporting and promoting sustainability.

(a) What are these reports called?

(b) Organisations in the UK are not legally obliged to produce these reports. Give a reason why a business might decide to report on how well they have met their sustainability targets.

7.3 Mitchell is an accountant who works in the Accounts Department of Alecon Ltd, a business that manufactures sportswear which they supply to high street retailers. He has been asked by the management of Alecon to review three ways of reducing costs and assess whether they are appropriate. Alecon has a policy of taking a sustainable approach to business wherever possible.

Look at the list of possible cost cutting methods below and for each one explain what sustainability issues the business may have to consider.

COST CUTTING METHODS
1 Move manufacturing to a factory in Bangladesh.
2 Close three of their four sales offices and have one central office which will result in a significant increase in business mileage for three quarters of its sales force.
3 Change supplier of packaging material from its current supplier that is based locally and uses recycled plastic, to a new overseas supplier who is offering Alecon a 25% discount.

7.4 Explain what is meant by the term reputational risk and how this is potentially affected by an organisation's attitude to Corporate Social Responsibility.

7.5 You are the most recently qualified member of staff at Delta & Co, a medium sized firm of accountants in Blistertown which has a total of 128 members of staff. Simon, the senior partner, has asked you to produce a document that explains to members of staff the key areas where they should encourage sustainability and sustainable development with their clients.

You should identify at least four points to include in this document.

ENCOURAGING SUSTAINABILITY

Answers to chapter activities

CHAPTER 1: PRINCIPLES OF PROFESSIONAL ETHICS

1.1   The International Ethics Standards Board for Accountants (IESBA), which is part of the International Federation of Accountants (IFAC).

1.2   ALL options apply

1.3   •   Integrity
  •   Objectivity
  •   Professional competence and due care
  •   Confidentiality
  •   Professional behaviour

1.4   Integrity

1.5   Objectivity

1.6   'A professional accountant who complies with the law and does not bring the accounting profession into disrepute is upholding the fundamental principle of **professional behaviour**'

CHAPTER 2: THREATS AND SAFEGUARDS TO FUNDAMENTAL ETHICAL PRINCIPLES

2.1   **(a)**   If Samantha accepts the new company as a client the fee income from this assignment will represent a substantial proportion of Samantha's total fee income. This could represent a self-interest threat to Samantha's objectivity as she could be reliant on the fees from Red News and its subsidiary.

  (b)   Samantha should not accept the additional work for Blue Media as she cannot reduce the self-interest threat she would face to an acceptable level.

2.2   'When providing consultancy services to an existing client, professional accountants may face a **self-review** threat to their fundamental ethical principles. They must ensure that they **do** make recommendations and **do not** make management decisions.

2.3   **(a)**   The two fundamental ethical principles that are most threatened by this situation are:

Integrity: if Hayley knows that the provision for doubtful debts was too low she has deliberately produced incorrect financial information which is both misleading to the users and dishonest.

Professional behaviour: knowingly allowing inaccurate and misleading information to be included in Andrew's financial statements breaches accounting regulations and consequently brings the accounting profession into disrepute.

(b)   Hayley faces an intimidation threat from Andrew's statement that 'it may not look good for you if the partners at Trott & Cook found out about this'.

(c)   Professional accountants should use their professional judgement to decide whether it is appropriate to accept gifts or hospitality from clients. Even if Hayley believes that she has not done anything wrong , the comments that Andrew has made in the thank you card, together with its significant value, mean that Hayley cannot accept the gift voucher from Andrew.

2.4   **(a)**   **Self-interest threat** – from the job offer at Headstyle Ltd.

Familiarity threat – from the length of time that Adrian has worked on the Headstyle assignment. Also the fact that the Managing Director has asked him not to mention the job offer until the assignment has been completed.

(b)   **Objectivity** – having a long and close working relationship with the management of Headstyle together with the offer of a senior position in the company will threaten Adrian's independence and hence his objectivity.

Professional behaviour – if Adrian does not declare his interest in Headstyle Ltd to his employers, Tahil & Emerson, then he could be accused of bringing the accounting profession into disrepute.

(c)   If Adrian does not intend to accept the job offer from Headstyle Ltd he should politely decline the offer from the Managing Director. If he is interested in the job offer he should explain the situation to a partner at Tahil & Emerson who can then decide whether to remove Adrian from the assignment or to put an additional level of review in for all the work that Adrian is responsible for.

2.5   **(a)**   **Self-interest threat** – Michael faces a self-interest threat to his fundamental ethical principles from the offer of the corporate box at the rugby. He must be careful to ensure that his judgement and behaviour are not influenced by this.

Intimidation threat – Jules is putting time pressure on Michael to complete the work within the next week.

(b)   **Objectivity** – as Michael has an interest in completing the work within the time available his objectivity may be threatened.

Professional competence and due care – if Michael is put under time pressure to complete the work allocated to him this may threaten his ability to carry it out competently and with appropriate due care.

(c) Michael should ensure that the offer is available to all members of staff ie he is not getting preferential treatment.

He should also make it clear to Jules that if he accepts the offer of the corporate box it will not influence any decisions he is asked to make.

Michael must ensure that he has adequate time to complete the work he has been allocated and if he does not then he should request additional help to complete the work or inform Jules that the work will be delayed.

2.6 Professional accountants who work in practice are more likely to face advocacy threats to their fundamental ethical principles if they are seen to support a client's point of view or to promote the client's position too strongly.

A professional accountant in business will be expected to support the legitimate goals and objectives of his/her employer and so would be expected to promote his/her employer's position. It is, therefore, unlikely that an accountant in business will face advocacy threats to his/her fundamental ethical principles.

CHAPTER 3: OBJECTIVITY AND THE RESOLUTION OF ETHICAL CONFLICT

3.1 (b) A principles-based approach

3.2 **(a)** False; **(b)** True

3.3 **(a)** Each of these clients is offering Wanda a gift. If she accepts these gifts this may cause a threat to her objectivity and it could influence decisions that she makes in relation to these clients and affect her independence.

(b) Wanda must use her professional judgement to decide in each of these cases whether she can accept the gifts from her clients.

- Provided she shares the contents of the hamper that Arthur has delivered with the staff at Ashby & Co she can probably accept this gift and thank Arthur for his kind words.

- The gift from Jayne is very generous and has not been offered to any other members of Wanda's team therefore she should decide that she cannot accept this gift and should thank Jayne for her kind offer but politely decline.

3.4 An inducement

(**Note**: the answer 'A bribe' would be acceptable if it can be proved that it influenced the accountant to do something favourable for the giver)

3.5 **(a)** For both Saul and Emma this situation threatens their objectivity and confidentiality.

(b) The offer that the Managing Director has made constitutes an inducement, which he is offering in an attempt to obtain confidential information. Saul cannot inform higher management in the organisation as the inducement has come from the Managing Director. Depending on the amount of pressure that he is putting on Saul the options available to him are:

- take legal advice
- inform a third party such as Saul's professional accounting body
- tell Emma as she would benefit from the inducement

3.6   10 years imprisonment and/or an unlimited fine.

3.7   **(a)**   **Objectivity** – acting for both clients with the same aim of securing the building land would be difficult for Terry. Even if he manages to remain independent there may be a perception by each of the two clients that he is favouring the other.

Confidentiality – it will be difficult for Terry to keep information about each client confidential. Again each client may perceive that he will use confidential information about it to benefit the other.

(b)   The process Terry should go through is:

- consider the relevant facts and ethical issues that this situation raises
- consider whether Parks & Co has established procedures for dealing with conflicts of interests between clients
- decide what alternative courses of action are available to him
- select the course of action that is most consistent with his fundamental principles
- discuss the issue with senior management at Parks & Co and document the issue and the discussion

(c)   If Terry decides to act for one of the clients he must consider what safeguards he can put in place so that his relationship with the other clients does not affect his professional judgement and his objectivity. These safeguards must also ensure that he does not breach the other client's confidentiality.

It should be noted that it is very unlikely that the threats to his fundamental ethical principles can be eliminated or reduced to an acceptable level. If this is the case then Terry will not be able to act for either of the clients.

3.8   **(a)**   Esther is employed by Goodrich Ltd and therefore is expected to be loyal to her employer; however she also has a duty of loyalty to her profession. She is being put under pressure by Sam to act contrary to accounting standards and overvalue the year-end inventory.

(b)   Esther should try and resolve the difference of opinion between her and Sam.

If this is not possible Esther should raise this issue with a more senior member of staff in the Accounts Department of Goodrich Ltd.

If Goodrich has a formal dispute resolution process Esther should follow this.

Esther can consult with her professional accounting body and take legal advice.

Ultimately if there are no other options open to her Esther may have to offer to resign from Goodrich Ltd.

CHAPTER 4: PROFESSIONAL AND TECHNICAL COMPETENCE

4.1 Any two of the following:
- reading professional journals
- enrolling on updating courses
- complying with continuing professional development (CPD) requirements for professional accountants

4.2 Erica should keep up to date with the following (one answer):
- changes in tax legislation
- changes in accounting regulations
- money laundering regulations
- financial reporting standards

Erica primarily provides services to small clients and, therefore the critical areas are regulations on tax, accounting and money laundering. Other areas such as auditing, company legislation, changes in ethical codes and changes in other areas of criminal law such as bribery and fraud are not critical areas for Erica's business.

4.3 Portas and Wright must ensure that their staff is kept up-to-date in the following (two answers):
- changes in auditing standards
- changes in accounting regulations
- money laundering regulations
- financial reporting standards
- changes in company legislation

Portas & Wright provides auditing services to its clients and prepares financial statements; therefore staff must be kept up-to-date on these critical areas. They must also be up-to-date on money laundering regulations. All firms of accountants have a duty to stay up-to-date with money laundering regulations. As Portas & Wright do not provide taxation services it is not critical for staff to receive regular taxation training.

4.4 Professional competence and due care.

4.5 Two of the following:
- obtain additional advice or training
- ensure that he has adequate time to carry out the work
- obtain assistance from someone with the necessary expertise
- consult with a more senior member of staff at Freemantle, independent experts or his professional accounting body

4.6 As Edwin has not completed a VAT Return before he must not mislead his employer, Frederickson & Brewer, about the extent of his expertise. He must explain that he would like to take responsibility for this work but will need some training from an experienced member of staff the first time he completes the VAT Return. His work should also be reviewed by a more senior member of staff until he is confident that he has the necessary expertise.

He should not complete the return without the necessary expertise.

4.7 • Breach of contract

• Professional negligence

4.8 Professional liability insurance

CHAPTER 5: CONFIDENTIALITY

5.1 False. The accountant's duty of confidentiality to a client extends to the period after the relationship has ended.

5.2 Robert has a duty of confidentiality to his client therefore he cannot disclose the financial information that Zeena has requested. In order for him to do so he would have to obtain authority from his client, which is very unlikely to be given.

5.3 Findlay should request authority from his client to disclose the information. Verbal authority is acceptable, but it would be better if this authority were given in writing. He can then give information to the office supplies company. He should include a disclaimer making it clear that this is for the use of the office supplies company only and is given purely to help them to make a decision about whether or not to supply goods on credit to your client. He should also explain that the information is given without any financial responsibility on the part of his firm of accountants.

5.4 Yes, Darren can disclose confidential information about Jessica to the National Crime Agency as Jessica's behaviour may be found to be money laundering.

5.5 An accountant has a professional duty to disclose confidential information to protect his/her **professional** interests in **legal proceedings**.

5.6 Notification

CHAPTER 6: CODES OF CONDUCT AND ORGANISATIONAL VALUES

6.1 No it will not be a statutory code. It has been created in response to guidelines produced by its trade organisation and so is a voluntary code.

Statutory codes must be created by legislation or regulation and will apply to a number of companies.

6.2 • being transparent with colleagues, customers and suppliers

• reporting financial and regulatory information clearly and on time

• being open and honest by indentifying when it is appropriate to accept and give gifts and hospitality

• paying suppliers a fair price and on time

• providing fair treatment, decent wages and good working conditions for employees

6.3 **(a)** cannot; **(b)** and **(c)** can

6.4 Felicity should consider the following:

- does she know all the facts surrounding the issue?
- does she have evidence to support these facts?
- she must follow her employer's internal procedures for reporting misconduct
- she must fully explain her concerns to management

6.5 **(a)** The Proceeds of Crime Act (POCA) 2002

The Terrorism Act 2000

The Money Laundering Regulations 2007

(b) An unlimited fine or a prison sentence of up to 14 years

(c) Money Laundering Reporting Officer (MLRO)

6.6 **(a)** Ashleigh should conduct CDD as this request for help to apply for an alcohol license is inconsistent with Ashleigh's current knowledge of her client, Voltec Ltd.

(b) Although Ashleigh has an established business relationship with Oscar, she will need to carry out appropriate CDD on Simeon. He is now the majority shareholder in the business and she must fully understand the nature of the business relationship between Oscar and Simeon.

(c) Ashleigh knows Helena James socially; however she must still carry out appropriate CDD as she is establishing a business relationship with her for the first time. She should verify her identity and find out what Helena wants from the business relationship with Ashleigh as it is currently Dennis who has asked her to complete Helena's tax return and hold the money for her to pay HMRC.

6.7 **(a)** Georgia must tell Edgar that she can no longer act for Opino Ltd. This is because the money that it has not paid to HMRC relating to the VAT error constitutes criminal property. By retaining it Opino Ltd could be charged with money laundering. Georgia must not tell Edgar why she can no longer act for Opino Ltd as this could constitute tipping off. As Georgia is a sole practitioner she must submit a Suspicious Activity Report (SAR) to the National Crime Agency (NCA).

(b) If Georgia continues to act for Opino then she is facilitating its retention of the money it should have paid to HMRC relating to the VAT error. In this situation she will be engaged in money laundering. She may also be guilty of the crime of failure to disclose.

(c) Once Joe becomes aware of the error he should report to NCA that he suspects Opino Ltd of money laundering. In these circumstances he will be protected from a claim of breach of confidentiality. As Joe is aware that he may also have been involved in money laundering he needs to make an authorised disclosure regarding Edgar's refusal to disclose the error to HMRC.

6.8 If Jake raises the issue with the management of Thompson Facilities he could be guilty of the offence of tipping off. Even if he does not intend to prejudice an investigation into possible money laundering by Thompson Facilities Ltd this offence could still apply.

CHAPTER 7: SUSTAINABILITY

7.1   **(a)**   The three objectives should be as stated below; however any sensible example of how a business can support the objective is acceptable.

---

1   Objective: **economic growth**

Examples:
- try to use locally sourced materials
- generate profit whilst still supporting social equality and without compromising the sustainability of the environment

2   Objective: **environmental protection**

Examples:
- recycling paper and printer cartridges used in an organisation's offices
- promoting car sharing schemes and cycle to work incentives

3   Objective: **social equality**

Example:
- ensure that businesses with which it trades provide reasonable pay and decent working conditions, particularly if they are based overseas
- sponsor local sporting events

(b)   'development that meets the needs of the present without compromising the ability of future generations to meet their own needs.'

7.2   **(a)**   Corporate Social Responsibility (CSR) Report.

(b)   The public and investors are keen to see a business's attitude to sustainability and will look more favourably on organisations which have made progress towards achieving their CSR goals.

7.3

COST CUTTING METHODS

1 Move manufacturing to a factory in Bangladesh.

Issues:

- ensure that the employees in the Bangladesh factory have decent working conditions and fair rates of pay
- assess the impact on staff in the UK of moving manufacturing to Bangladesh such as redundancy
- consider the effect on the environment, such as increased CO_2 emissions, of transporting the goods from Bangladesh to the UK

2 Close three of their four sales offices and have one central office which will result in a significant increase in business mileage for three quarters of its sales force.

Issues:

- consider the effect on the environment of the increased travelling for its sales staff
- consider the effect on the working conditions of the sales staff if they have to travel further and longer during the course of their working day
- quantify the reduction in the costs of power and other running costs of centralising the sales office to one location

3 Change supplier of packaging material from its current supplier that is based locally and uses recycled plastic to a new overseas supplier who is offering a 25% discount.

Issues:

- investigate the sustainability credentials of the new supplier to see whether they use recycled materials and offer decent working conditions to their staff
- consider the effect on local employment of sourcing the material from overseas
- assess the effect on the environment of the potential new supplier transporting the packaging materials greater distances

---

7.4   Reputational risk is the risk of loss resulting from damage to an organisation's reputation.

An organisation will include its sustainability targets in its Corporate Social Responsibility (CSR). When it produces a CSR report this will show its progress towards these targets. There is a risk to an organisation's reputation if it reports negative results. However the fact that a business is prepared to report its progress towards its sustainability targets and CSR will have a positive effect on its reputation.

7.5   The answer should cover four of the six points detailed below.

ENCOURAGING SUSTAINABILITY

1   **Products and services** – explain to clients that they should try to ensure that their products or services are produced from sustainably resourced materials

2   **Customers** – help clients to supply to their customers in a sustainable manner

3   **Employees** – encourage clients to provide good working conditions for their staff

4   **The workplace** – suggest green policies that clients can introduce including recycling and conservation of energy

5   **The supply chain** – encourage clients to research the sustainability credentials of their suppliers

6   **Business functions and processes** – explain to client management that they should constantly review the way in which they operate to ensure it continues to support and encourage sustainability and sustainable development

---

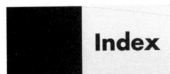

Index

for your notes

for your notes

for your notes

for your notes

for your notes

for your notes

for your notes